MASTER YOUR MORTGAGE

Contact information for Kick Start Publishing Inc:
info@kickstartpublishing.com

ISBN: 978-1-7779495-0-1 (paperback)
ISBN: 978-1-7779495-2-5 (hardcover)
ISBN: 978-1-7779495-3-2 (ebook)

Ordering Information:
Special discounts are available on quantity purchases by corporations, associations, and others. For details, contact info@kickstartpublishing.com, #250-997 Seymour St, Vancouver, BC, Canada, V6B 3M1

BRIGHTON GBARAZIA

MASTER YOUR MORTGAGE

WHAT THE **BANK** WON'T TELL YOU ABOUT BUYING THE RIGHT HOME

CONTENTS

I have been blessed with an abundance of riches. My first was being born to parents who gave me so much love. My parents provided me with all I ever required to succeed in this life. My sister and brother kept me honest and picked me up whenever I needed it. They showed me love and taught me the importance of empathy and family. As though that wasn't enough, I managed to strike gold again and was blessed with the love of my life and my best friend who has been by my side since I was practically a kid. She helped me develop into the man I am today and to continue working toward being in the future. She's my reminder of what's really important in this life. That's the thing about riches: It's often the most obvious riches that we miss in life.

INTRODUCTION

Mortgages are one of the most talked about aspect of purchasing a home, yet the mortgage debt is often not talked about. It's hard to speak proudly about taking on $716,585 in mortgage debt, which was the national average home price in Canada as of October 2021 according to The Canadian Real Estate Association (CREA).[1] So, the dollar amount of a mortgage is usually hush-hush. Instead, most of us opt to discuss rates and which bank or mortgage professional helped us secure the mortgage as a way to avoid discussing the actual debt.

Indeed, if anyone should start questioning you about the actual mortgage debt, you quickly change the topic to the beauty of the home. You talk about all the emotionally positive qualities that the home will bring you and your family, such as the fact it's near a great school district, how close it is to your friends and family, easy access to the highways, or closeness to your work. But sometimes, that's not enough to stop those nosy friends of yours, and you have to bring out the secret weapon. What's the secret

---

1   "National Statistics," The Canadian Real Estate Association (CREA), November 15, 2021, https://creastats.crea.ca/en-CA/.

weapon? Take them on a tour of that fantastic kitchen and spa bathroom with a rain showerhead that feels like the water is coming directly from heaven. You know that will shut them up. How could you put a price on such happiness?

A home, in my opinion, is one of the most emotionally charged purchases anyone will make. Emotions and good financial decisions are like an oxymoron—they don't go together. The worse part about emotional purchases is you constantly use your logical thinking to justify your illogical financial decisions. A home is an expensive purchase where mistakes made can have long-lasting impact. For most people, the quality of their life is determined by their mortgage debt, and I'm not talking about your rate or mortgage product. That's why it is crucially important to spend a lot of your time understanding your mortgage debt and what the implications of the debt will have on the quality of life for you and those you care about.

At times, what you are about to read might make you uncomfortable, embarrassed, upset, excited, or hopeful depending on where you are in your mortgage journey. Regardless of the emotions this book might bring up, I encourage you to read it in its entirety. We cannot change the past, but we can create the future we want by learning from our past. For those of you who are willing to learn and make the necessary changes after reading this book, you will have a path forward. I will not only provide information that will help you understand the mortgage approval process, but for those of you who already have a mortgage, I will provide options on how to reduce your mortgage burden and cut years off your mortgage with simple concepts.

This book is made up of three parts. Part 1 will provide you some context about me and my experiences working for some of Canada's largest banks. Part 2 is the reason you bought this book. I will discuss "all things mortgages," such as how the bank approves you for a mortgage and what banks and lenders look for in a mortgage application. You will be able to practice your understanding of these concepts with actual cases that I worked on during my time at the bank. I will also share with you what actually happened with those cases. Part 3 is a bonus section. In this section, I will share what I have learned about wealth creation and working toward financial independence.

To get the full benefit from this book, all parts should be read together and in its entirety, as it will be incomplete if any parts are read in isolation.

Now, let's address what this book is not. It's not a real estate investing book. This book was written for individuals or families who want to purchase a home as their principal residence. While I do have experience in the investment side of real estate, the target audience for this book isn't real estate investors. I didn't want to write a real estate book because there is an abundance of great real estate books out there, and I didn't have anything new to add. However, there are far fewer books that focus just on the individual looking to buy a home as a primary residence and that explain the mortgage approval process. Furthermore, there are far fewer books focused around the Canadian mortgage process, as many books on the market are U.S.-based.

The topics I write about in this book are based on my experiences with the subject matter. I have done my best to ensure it's accurate, but please be mindful that mortgage rules change frequently. Therefore, my approach isn't to turn you into an underwriter, but rather provide you an idea of how the system works. The specifics will change over time, but I want you to understand how the system is designed and how you get your mortgage.

As you read this book, you might be tempted to think I am smarter than you, and I have it all figured out. I do not have anything figured out, and I surround myself with people who remind me of that. Most of my knowledge was acquired through painful mistakes on my part. Therefore,

I know these pitfalls not because I am smarter than you; rather, I might have a little more experience with real estate and have made a lot of the same mistakes you might have. Keep that in mind.

I simply want the best for you and those you care about and really want you to wake up to the reality of the true cost of your mortgage, which you might fail to see. My challenge in writing this book is trying to get you to be less emotional about your home in hopes you can see beyond the high emotional attachment you have with your home.

Now, with that out of the way, let us begin the story and journey.

The only thing an
imperfect human being
fears more than their
own imperfections
is another imperfect
human being who's
perfectly comfortable
with their own
imperfections and
limitations.

Part 1

Uncovering the Bank's Secrets

CHAPTER 1

AN UNINTENTIONAL JOURNEY

My family and I immigrated to Canada in the late 90s. Our journey to Canada wasn't one of seeking to come to Canada intentionally, but rather events outside my parents' control put us on a path that would eventually lead us to Canada.

Before we arrived, my family spent three years in a refugee camp in the Republic of Benin, a country located in West Africa. I was extremely young during this time, but not so young that I did not recall my time in the camp. From what I can recall, the refugee camp was not what most of you might be thinking, at least not early on. My family shared a room with another family from the same town as my parents. As a kid, I recall my life being mostly normal. I had friends to hang out with, my family was with me, and we all went to church on Sunday. Nevertheless, I knew my parents were worried about something when we left Nigeria. As a kid, though, I didn't understand the significance of their worry other than what my parents told me, which was that we were moving. But as the years went on in the camp, more people who were from my parents' town kept coming. From a kid's perspective, I just saw more new friends coming to the neighborhood. My simple worry was having to leave my friends. I didn't understand that we were fleeing for our safety.

My parents left their place of birth for many of the same reasons most refugees leave their home country: conflict. In my parents' case, it was an economic conflict around resources. My parents are from a small tribe in Nigeria called Ogoni. An overseas oil company had a pipeline that ran through the village. At the time, the local residents complained that the pipeline had some issues and was contaminating the water supply. The residents protested to raise their concerns, but given the economic benefits of oil, the government at the time didn't want to listen to the locals' concerns. A conflict that could have been resolved through dialogue ended up becoming a conflict where thousands would die unnecessarily.

Local leaders of the Ogoni people were killed to send a message to the community. The Ogoni people feared for their safety and started to flee their home country. At the time, my family did not live where the conflict was occurring. We lived in one of Nigeria's largest cities, called Lagos. However, the conflict became a concern for my father given he was Ogoni, and my father's and mother's parents along with their extended family lived in the area of the conflict. To protect their kids, my parents decided we could not stay in Nigeria and made what I now realize was a painful decision for both of them. They left a place they knew, the family they knew, the country they were born in and loved, friends they knew, and decided to protect their family at any cost. But like all decisions in life, there's always a cost, and unfortunately, my parents paid a personal cost to ensure their kids would live a life without violence. We eventually would leave the refugee camp upon being sponsored by Canada. After a few years in Canada, I finally realized how traumatic those years were for my parents.

Few ordinary people anywhere in the world knew of the trauma. My family's distress happened before social media delivered its power to share information. To know of the story, you would have had to have been in Nigeria or have known someone very close to the event. As a result, it wasn't a story most in Canada knew much about. My father spent his early years in Canada telling anyone we met our story in an effort to let people know what was happening back in Nigeria. He hated seeing his country in conflict.

My father isn't a man who believed in extreme positions. He believed that extreme positions box people in, preventing them from taking the right action. I take the same approach to my life. While a particular oil company failed to listen to local concerns about its business operations, that doesn't mean I think all oil companies are bad. I buy oil and appreciate it has made some of the products and other things I enjoy. I have friends and family who work in this industry, and some are Ogoni and Nigerians.

In fact, crude and gas petroleum products made up 84.1% of Nigeria's export in 2019.[2] Therefore, since I want Nigeria to succeed on the economic stage, I want them to utilize their resource to its full advantage, much like Canada does. But saying that also means such success cannot come at the expense of the people who ultimately own the resource and for whom it should benefit. After all, shouldn't all businesses only operate as long as the citizens in the area continue to see the benefit of such operations?

LESSONS OF MY FATHER

My father passed away in his early 40s. Though he is no longer here physically, his lessons along with my parents' journey to Canada have

---

2   "What does Nigeria export?" The Observatory of Economic Complexity (OEC), 2019, https://oec.world/en/visualize/tree_map/hs92/export/nga/all/show/2019/.

taught me two important truths, which I have incorporated into my life today.

The first is to avoid extreme positions as they often result in your taking extreme actions that can lead to deadly consequences simply to uphold your position or belief. Extreme positions prevent you from being able to compromise in that doing so makes you feel as though you've lost or given up on what you stood for.

Second, I spend more time judging my own actions and less time judging others, which helps to foster an empathic approach to create a pathway to forgiveness. As humans, we are good at pointing out when another human's action doesn't match their value or words. But while we are quick to judge others, we are awful at holding ourselves accountable. We avoid pointing the lens at ourselves because when we do so we realize we are just as imperfect as the other human beings we criticize. I've come to learn if we spend more time looking at our own actions and behavior, it helps us understand we are not perfect, and therefore, we're more likely to accept that others can't be perfect. It's a complicated world, and we are complicated people; therefore, solutions to problems are likely to be complicated.

CHAPTER 2

FROM A CASH SYSTEM TO A CREDIT SYSTEM

My parents' initial financial experience in Canada wasn't great. They came from a cash-based financial system and society, which meant my parents were used to paying for everything in cash, in full. Canada was a credit-based financial system where people don't pay for things in full and certainly not by cash. Adjusting from a cash-based system to credit-based system was already going to be a difficult transition for them, but their experience was further complicated with poor financial advice they got.

Watching my parent's frustration with the financial system was one of the driving forces behind why I wanted to work in the financial industry, specifically in personal finance. I wanted to help people with money and provide them the advice my parents didn't get. I enjoyed learning about money and wanted to learn how money worked. The financial industry, therefore, seemed like a natural fit for me in which to pursue a career, which is what I did.

I started my financial career not as an advisor but rather as a collections officer, which was my first job after I finished university. I worked for one of the major banks in Canada in the auto collections' side of the business. I was the person who would call people trying to get them to make their missed car payments. I was uncomfortable in the role at first because I didn't like calling people and telling them to pay up. Collection is a difficult role because you start off wanting to believe people, and you end up not trusting anyone or anything they say. It turns your trust in humanity upside down. Sometimes, I would talk to a person who had to choose between car payments or groceries for their family. Other times, I would talk to someone who didn't make his payment because they were going on vacation with friends.

Then there was the time I got a call from a guy who was making $120,000 a year and decided he didn't want to make the car payment anymore. He had pulled his truck off the side of the highway when he called me to advise his monthly car payments were unfair. Sitting at my desk, I agreed with him that his payments where high, but then asked why he agreed to make a $1,000 a month truck payment in the first place. Silence proceeded until I decided to stop the awkwardness and advised him of his next payment date.

I could write an entire book just on excuses people provide for not making their car payments. The collection role was challenging because after you are lied to so much, you just accept the role of collecting the money regardless of their story. It's the only way to do your job really.

I eventually became really good at the collection job while not losing myself. I learned to strike a balance with customers, and they started to keep my payment arrangements. I believe they kept making the payments because they felt I sincerely wanted to help them, which I did. But the role still wasn't the type of job I wanted. After some time, a financial advisor job came up. It was an entry-level position, but it would get me into the financial advisor world. I applied and got the job. I was really excited about it as finally I would get to talk to people and help them reach their financial goals.

Upon becoming an advisor, I discovered the reality of the job wasn't as I had envisioned. I had an internal conflict within myself about the role. I wanted to focus on understanding people's wants and needs and then make recommendations to help them reach their goal. I wasn't interested in selling financial products, but the steps I wanted to take to offer advice were backwards. I constantly felt I had to sell the product first, regardless of whether the client needed it.

At every meeting I had to sell, even though sometimes advising is simply talking down clients from selling when the market is crashing without any product being transacted. But at the bank, it was always product first, product second, product third, and when in doubt, throw another product at the client. I started to hate the role a few months in as I felt I had entered a sales role where financial advising wasn't the core of the business.

THE SMALL PRINT

After some time, I thought perhaps I felt that way because I was in an entry role, and since I wasn't knowledgeable enough to discuss complex financial matters in my role, selling of product was all I was able to do. I decided to look for a more complex role that was focused first on financial advising with little selling of products. I lucked out and landed another role that I thought would be perfect.

On paper, the job description hit all the boxes. I even asked all the right questions during my interview to ensure it was the job I thought I was applying for. The manager and everyone said all the right things to me about "client first and product only if it fits a client's needs." But I soon learned it all would come back to selling.

It wasn't that I couldn't sell, but so often, I felt selling just for the sake of selling was wrong. When it comes to money, my brain operates from a non-emotional place. My business philosophy was to treat clients the way I would treat my parents, and I couldn't understand selling something that was not the best financial tool to meet a person's financial goals. Still, I had acquired clients who had multiple mutual funds, and I couldn't understand why. Neither could they. I started to connect the dots when I discovered I was their fourth advisor, and each advisor before me sold mutual funds to meet the advisor's annual target. Learning that I was giving my clients the second-best product and advice frustrated me, to put it lightly.

I eventually decided to move away from the financial advisor role as it became clear I wouldn't be able to do what I wanted to do or how I wanted to do it unless I ran my own financial firm, and I wasn't in a position to do that. Eventually, I moved on to mortgage underwriter. However, the conversations I would have during my time as a financial advisor would prove to be valuable in assisting my understanding of homeownership when I was ready to purchase my first home.

CHAPTER 3

THE HIDDEN COSTS OF HOMEOWNERSHIP

A home is so much more than just an investment or shelter. The benefits that a home provide are not just the investment return or its protection from the harsh environment. At its core, a home is a place to build and create lasting memories with those you care for and love. This strong emotional pull that a home has is what makes it such a complicated and difficult transaction to do right, even for those who know all the emotional trappings of homeownership.

The situation was no different when my wife and I decided to buy our first home. Since my family had rented in Canada up until my mother bought our first family home after my father passed away, I always wanted to own a home. I especially wanted to own a single-family detached home. I wanted a nice yard, big bedrooms, nice deck, and a house that looked impressive to other people. But our budget couldn't afford most of those features.

When we started our home purchase journey, I was working as a financial advisor. I had spoken to a lot of my clients who were homeowners, and naturally, I would work my homeownership intent into our meetings to seek their advice. I spoke to individuals and families who had been long-time homeowners. As I spoke to many of my clients, I noticed two things shared among the most successful homeowners. Those who bought their home primarily to provide shelter for their family were extremely focused on their mortgage debt level. They worked extremely hard to eliminate their mortgage debt during their most active working years. The second thing I noticed was they continued to stress that I understand the complete cost of homeownership, which they didn't know initially, and wanted me to be fully aware of before getting a home. As they shared their reflections on their homeownership journey, I started to feel less excited as it became apparent that buying a home wasn't just about covering the mortgage payments.

The ability to be able to discuss homeownership with actual homeowners, who had gone through the process and were at a point in their lives where they could be honest with me about what they really felt and experienced, is ultimately what I credit with our first home purchase being more successful than if I had not had those conversations. They didn't know it, but they were allowing me to learn from their mistakes, which allowed me to avoid the costliest mistake that first-time homebuyers often neglect or have to learn by making those mistakes themselves.

Before I started those conversations, which took place a few years before we actually planned to purchase our home, I was extremely emotional about buying a home. Since I grew up renting in Canada, I always felt as though renting was a reflection on me for not being successful. Growing up, I felt that people looked at my parents differently because we rented. I wanted a home for myself to show people I was successful and didn't want to get the looks people often gave to my parents when they said they rented. I didn't realize that was one of the strong emotional reasons why

I wanted a home so badly. I wanted to use my home as a means to show people that I was successful. I wouldn't have realized it if I didn't have conversations with clients who were long-time homeowners. They started to show me that a home should be a place you raise your family and that the best way to achieve it was to keep your eye on the mortgage debt.

When my wife and I were finally ready to buy a home, I had done some self-reflection on why I really wanted a home and spent some time understanding that a home isn't something I should use as a means of trying to show people I was successful. Therefore, when we started looking for our home, we stayed focus on the mortgage debt and really asked ourselves if that mortgage debt would allow us to live the life we wanted at that time while enabling us to invest in the future. I knew from speaking to my clients that the bigger the mortgage debt, the fewer the options we would have then and in the future as more income would be required to service that debt.

UNDERSTANDING THE COMPLETE COST OF HOMEOWNERSHIP

One of the biggest things that all my experienced homeowner-clients expressed to me was when they got their first home, they didn't really understand all the associated costs. They advised that the one-time costs, such as closing charges, inspection, or appraisal fee, were easy to understand as they were something they had to pay before moving in. However, they related that some of the ongoing costs after owning the home were shocking and completely unanticipated. Therefore, I made sure when we started our home search that I accounted for all the costs of operating our home (one-time costs and ongoing expenses) in addition to the mortgage payment. To truly know what we could afford, I made sure I knew all the expenses we would be required to make. I identified the main recurring expenses we needed to cover in addition to the mortgage payments:

- → Strata payment (if we bought a condo or townhouse)
- → Electricity
- → Natural gas
- → Property taxes
- → Property insurance
- → City services, such as water/garbage
- → Regular maintenance (roof repair, gutter cleaning, roof replacement, repainting, etc.)

If you were not aware of those costs and if they aren't fully accounted for, you're likely to feel financial stress when you discover them. For example, for one listing we looked at, I had to contact the city as the house ad listed the previous year's tax amount that turned out to be much lower than the current year tax amount. Information like that one item is crucial if you are on a tight budget. Verification of such expenses rests with the prospective purchaser.

Furthermore, ongoing costs were also important for us to know in order to understand our excess cash flow situation. Your excess cash flow is the difference between your total monthly income subtracted from your total monthly expenses. For example, if your monthly income is $5,000 and your monthly expenses are $3,000, then your monthly excess cash flow is $2,000. What I learned as an advisor and confirmed by my clients' conversations was to keep our fixed expenses as low as possible to provide more excess cash flow to do the things that made us happy. It sounds simple, but often when you are starting your homeownership journey, you are not made aware of all the associated costs; therefore, the excess cash flow you think you have is actually much lower.

Before we went to look at a home, I did the pre-work on the total housing costs of the home to see if it was even worth viewing. To obtain some of the ongoing cost numbers, I had to estimate them or call city staff to obtain the information about the property. I would use our realtor to start, but I always confirmed the information through a neutral third party or source to ensure the estimated numbers were not super-low to make the purchase look good.

Understanding the total cost of a potential home we wanted to buy compared to our budget helped us greatly in two ways. First, we didn't even look at a home that didn't fit our budget because we knew it wouldn't work. Second, by doing our homework we avoided the emotional traps that often get first-time homebuyers, which is to fall in love with a home and then do whatever it takes to make the numbers work. Our approach reduced the likelihood of that ploy happening as we couldn't fall in love if we didn't even see it.

Doing the analysis of the home costs before we even saw it also gave us more confidence when looking at the home, as we knew if we liked the home, we could make an offer right away as the numbers already met our requirement. That benefit was critical as it reduced arguments between us regarding what we were comfortable to spend. Instead, we were focused on what we liked or didn't like about the home in terms of aesthetics and features, which is a huge deal in your ultimate happiness about your home purchase.

ANTICIPATING FUTURE COSTS BEYOND HOMEOWNERSHIP COST

Understanding the complete cost of homeownership isn't just about understanding the total housing expenses. In speaking to my clients, they would share stories of their mortgage at 18% and how they worked two jobs to cover mortgage payments. Some would share how they had to take out debt to cover their kids' education and other family expenses due to most of their money going to cover housing payments. The stories they shared themed around the fact that covering your housing expenses wasn't the only cost involved in homeownership. They were saying how covering their monthly housing expenses sometimes reduced their ability to deal with other life events that occurred. They were saying to me, while you are young today, life will change for you as you get older. Things you never thought you might want to do might become of interest to you; therefore, pay attention to your mortgage debt and ensure the home you buy can give you as much flexibility to change or deal with additional expenses that life might bring. They were advising me to think about where my life is today and where it might be tomorrow, and then ask myself if my mortgage debt will give me more flexibility in the future or restrict my ability to handle future financial obligations.

As I thought more about our purchase, I realized that the excess cash flow was extremely important as my clients were essentially saying there will be more expenses to come in the future, and the more free cash flow available, the better the chances of being able to deal with it. The future wasn't something I had considered really, as I was focused on just ensuring we could cover the total housing cost of the home. I hadn't really thought about lifestyle cost of the home, which ultimately made living enjoyable. If we could cover our housing cost but didn't have extra to spend on the things that made us happy, it wouldn't be as enjoyable of an experience to be a homeowner.

Homeownership is much more than just covering housing cost. It is also about ensuring you could have the lifestyle you want. While I understood the impact that mortgage debt can have on our desired type of lifestyle, such as continuing to travel and saving toward retirement, I didn't know how our lifestyle would change as we aged. To accommodate longer-term contingencies, we had to keep our mortgage debt low while seeking a home with future income-producing potential. With that new understanding, we focused our housing search on finding a home that had the potential to build a secondary suite to potentially rent it out in the future. Finding something within our budget that met those criteria also meant that I would be driving roughly an hour and a half each way to work.

I didn't intend on having to share our home with someone else as I wanted the home for us alone, and while from a financial standpoint the answer was straightforward, emotionally I struggled at first. However, we were more willing to pursue that type of housing because we were living in a basement suite ourselves at the time. We realized buying a principal residence and renting the self-contained basement suite wasn't that bad as long as we spent the time to find the right people to share our space with, which I will share my experience as a landlord in Part 3 of the book.

I believe our first home purchase went well largely because of the amount of pre-work that we did before we even started looking for a home. As a result, we were clear about our homeownership objective and were better able to put in place a system to ensure we didn't buy a home we loved emotionally but put us in a financially difficult position.

CHAPTER 4

A BROKEN MORTGAGE SYSTEM

W hile I spent a lot of time understanding the true cost of homeownership before making our first purchase, I found the mortgage approval process extremely frustrating due to the lack of information that was provided to me about our mortgage debt.

When we went through the mortgage process, I found the information I presented in the previous chapter wasn't communicated to me. For the most part, information that was requested from me was simply collected to facilitate my mortgage approval. For example, the lender wanted to know what the taxes were for the property in order to qualify us but didn't talk to me about budgeting for that amount or why including the cost in our budget was important. I was asked to get a property insurance quote, but again no one actually sat down to discuss with me the importance of ongoing costs related to the home. All the information collected from me was simply to move the application forward to either advise me of our approval or decline. Our initial mortgage application was declined.

The individual who was assisting me advised that the lender declined our application as our total debt service ratio (TDS) was out of line. They explained our TDS was above the lender's requirement but provided no real explanation regarding what total debt service ratio was and how exactly we had failed to meet it.

We eventually got approved through a local credit union. I was a little confused as to why one lender declined us and another approved us. I asked, but again no one really gave me a clear reason. The answer was simply that lenders sometimes have different guidelines and that this one had approved us.

After we signed the mortgage document, that was pretty much it. No real conversation around the mortgage debt, budgeting, or housing expenses. No one seemed to care to explain the true cost of homeownership to me. I recall thinking, why are we not discussing the mortgage debt more? Everyone seemed to either just want to give us an approval and move on, or when it was a decline, no real explanation as to why.

At the time, I didn't pay much attention, and honestly didn't care. See, after we got the first decline, I was surprised and worried we would need more down payment, which we didn't have. When we finally got an approval, I didn't want to discuss anything and was just glad we were approved.

Once the homeownership process starts, you get a pathway of seeking an approval regardless of the long-term financial implication. Our saving grace was, thankfully, those conversations I had with bank clients that helped us create a system and protected us even when we were not getting the complete information around homeownership and mortgage debt from the financial institution.

But something didn't feel right after we got the mortgage. I kept asking myself why the individuals we worked with didn't spend more time planning with us or explaining our mortgage debt. I thought perhaps the reason the people we worked with didn't spend any time explaining things was because the lender and their underwriters did this on the back end. Therefore, I assumed at the time that they gave us the approval because they knew we could afford it and likely were using similar housing expenses explained in the previous chapter and came to the conclusion that we could afford our home.

However, when I got my first mortgage underwriting role, I quickly realized that assumption was not the case at all. I realized a lender's approval for a mortgage is not the same thing as their saying you can afford the mortgage you've been approved for. Lenders are in the business of risk underwriting, which means their focus isn't about affordability, but rather risk mitigation to provide a reasonable return for the level of risk they're taking. As a mortgage underwriter, I could approve a deal that wasn't financially sound for the individual situation because I could mitigate or eliminate the chances of losing money on the loan.

I would come to learn that lenders don't take into account the full cost of homeownership when they provide their approval. They only took a small portion of the costs associated with a home. Lenders only take 50% of the condo or strata fees, for example, when qualifying for a mortgage. That way of underwriting works for the lender to be able to provide a higher loan amount, which generates higher interest payments. However, that allowance can cause financial stress to the borrower if they do not understand that they have been given a higher loan amount due to the lender's say-so yet will be required to pay 100% of that cost after the mortgage funds.

Perhaps the most shocking discovery I made as an underwriter is that mortgage loans are approved based on an individual's gross income, yet the homeowner is expected to make payments based on their after-tax net income. For example, if you had a gross income of $60,000, the lender would take that income to qualify you for your mortgage loan amount. Let's assume your after-tax income is $50,000. The lender approved you based on your gross income of $60,000, which at the time of your application they know it's not your take-home pay since taxes likely are withheld. Therefore, you essentially start the mortgage journey by getting approved for more money than you actually should.

The approval of mortgages based on gross income isn't a bad thing or the sole reason why people might be "house poor." However, the reason that approach to mortgage approval often results in people being stretched financially is because most people do not know that's how the bank approves them for a mortgage. The knowledge gap that homeowners have in how their mortgage is approved often means people are signing up for loans that they are approved for based on an income level they actually do not take home.

However, no one forces the homeowner to take on the mortgage loan. Smart prospective homeowners need to do their own due diligence to determine what appropriate mortgage debt they want to take on. But such thoroughness is not an easy step when you're buying something that's so emotional, such as a home. Furthermore, first-time homeowners need more education as they tend to have the least amount of experience regarding true homeownership costs while dealing with the high emotional pull their first home has. The 2019 Mortgage Consumer Survey, which is completed by first-time and repeat homeowners done by Canada Mortgage and Housing Corporation (CMHC), found that 33% of homebuyers advised they did not have a monthly budget in place before they bought their home.[3] It also found 59% of buyers confirmed the need to reduce their non-essential spending after getting their home. Entertainment (66%), vacation (55%), and food (44%) were the top three non-essential expenditures being reduced.[4] Clearly, we all need to spend more time understanding our mortgage debt and how it's related to our daily life.

In Part 2, you will learn about the mortgage process that will help you better understand the mortgage approval system. It isn't meant to be a comprehensive homeownership or mortgage approval guide but a means to have a bigger conversation about homeownership while reducing your mortgage knowledge gap.

3   "The State of Homebuying in Canada: 2019 CMHC Mortgage Consumer Survey," Canada Mortgage and Housing Corporation (CMHC), November 14, 2019, https://www.cmhc-schl. gc.ca/en/professionals/housing-markets-data-and-research/housing-research/surveys/mortgage-consumer-surveys/survey-results-2019.

4   Ibid.

Part 2

Understanding the Mortgage Approval Process

CHAPTER 5

THE TRUE DEFINITION
OF CAPITAL

When I approached our first home purchase, I had some basic knowledge on the loan approval since I worked at a bank. I knew we had to have a certain credit score, but I didn't really understand the mortgage approval process. I didn't know anything about the 5 C's, as I'm about to explain to you, as I was in the sales-advising side of the bank. Upon becoming an underwriter, I learned about the mortgage-approval system that was used to underwrite mortgages and would come to learn that mortgage applications are not just approved or declined solely because you have poor credit or meet a certain credit score. There is a system behind how lenders review mortgage applications, and they look at multiple aspects and not just a single element. Great underwriting should be a win-win situation for the prospective borrower and lender. There are a whole host of things that go into trying to achieve this win-win outcome. For lenders, having strong underwriting guidelines and policy is critical for their success while providing excellent service to their customers. Any good lender will invest money into the training of staff and development of a strong underwriting policy and guidelines. The ultimate goal for a lender is to have a consistent underwriting process that results in a profitable mortgage business with minimum or manageable risk exposure that the lender is willing to take on to achieve those profits.

To achieve that balance, most lenders encourage anyone underwriting to understand what's known as the 5 C's of credit, which consist of a set of criteria to assess the creditworthiness of a borrower. When assessing a borrower against the five criteria, a lender can better determine how strong a potential borrower's overall mortgage application is.

The 5 C's of credit in no particular order are credit, character, capital, collateral, and capacity. A lender will assess a borrower in each area to get a clear sense of the strengths and weaknesses of the borrower's application. To understand the mortgage process, you have to understand the basics of the 5 C's of credit as that's where lenders will start their underwriting process and your application.

CREDIT

Credit refers to your credit bureau reports to see if you have a good repayment history and credit score. The lender is looking at your entire credit profile, mostly relying on information you provide, your credit bureau, and what it finds that's in the public domain. Most lenders will focus their effort on information found through your credit bureau, but just know they also do their own investigation. Payments that are made late will impact your credit score and will make the lender view you as less creditworthy.

I have an entire section in the book on understanding your credit score and will go into far more detail on this topic. For now, simply know it's one of the 5 C's that lenders look at.

CHARACTER

Character refers to the borrower's overall application submission. It's not about if you're a nice person or a mean person. It's about how you've behaved with credit you've had, if any. The lender is trying to get an idea of how credit mature you are to get an idea of how likely you are to meet your debt obligations.

Lenders also look at how honest you are in your application. If you lied about something in your application, a lender is more likely to view you as less trustworthy. It's important then to keep in mind that in addition to your credit history, the lender is also looking at how honest you are about your application and intention.

For example, did you previously default on a mortgage but intentionally failed to disclose that to the lender? Did you have a bankruptcy, but in your initial application to the lender you didn't mention it even though you knew? Character is mostly about your credit profile but can extend to your personal attributes such as honesty and trustworthiness with respect to your application submission.

INSIDER TIP:

It's best to be honest on your application submission with a lender. Most lenders don't expect people to be perfect, but they want to know the risk exposure. If they know the risk exposure, they can work with you to try and find a solution to mitigate it. However, a lender is less likely to try to find a solution if they feel you intentionally lied about the application details provided.

CAPITAL

Capital looks at a borrower's cash requirement to qualify for the loan. In the mortgage business, capital is usually referring to the minimum down payment required for your application. For example, the minimum down payment for an insured mortgage in Canada, at the time of this writing, is 5% of the purchase price.[5] That factor means if you are trying to get a mortgage loan that's considered an insured mortgage, then you will have to have at least 5% of the purchase price available for down payment regardless of meeting the other credit requirements. If you don't have enough down payment money to facilitate your application, the application is unlikely to proceed as you haven't met the minimum required by the lender to consider your application. Lenders will usually accept a variety of capital down payment sources such as cash, equity, or gifted down payment from a family member.

Additionally, capital can also be used to determine a borrower's fallback position should they lose their job or find themselves having difficulties making payments. A lender will look at what assets you have in order to deal with financial challenges that might occur during your mortgage term. One such tool a lender might use is known as your net worth statement. An individual's net worth is determined by simply taking all the individual's assets (cash, investments, property, etc.) subtracted by all associated debts (mortgages, credit card, line of credit, etc.).[6] The difference between the two numbers is referred to as your personal net worth, which can be positive or negative.

Someone who has a strong net worth is in a better fallback position than someone who has a negative net worth. But having a positive net worth isn't all a lender is looking for. A lender is also looking at what type of assets makes up your net worth or lack of net worth.

---

5   "Mortgage Default Insurance (CMHC Insurance)," Ratehub, updated January 11, 2021, https://www.ratehub.ca/cmhc-mortgage-insurance.

6   Jean Folger, "How to Calculate Your Tangible Net Worth," Investopedia, updated June 8, 2021, https://www.investopedia.com/articles/pf/13/calculating-your-tangible-net-worth.asp.

For example, let's say two people have an identical net worth of $150,000. The net worth of individual A is made up of $150,000 in stocks. The net worth of person B is entirely based on their real estate holdings, which provides them with equity of $150,000. Assuming we know nothing else about either people and they are seeking a $100,000 mortgage, if capital was the only factor the lender is looking at, which individual would you feel better about lending your money to, A or B?

If you said A, I would agree with you, though both would qualify for the loan if capital was the only criteria. A is a stronger applicant based on the makeup of net worth. A's fallback position is based on $150,000 in liquid assets. If something did go wrong, A could sell the stock investment and pay out the lender in full. B also has a strong fallback position; however, B's fallback is not as strong as it's not as liquid as A's stock investment—meaning it's harder for person B to access that capital.

Capital and liquidity are important aspects to determine and know about before starting your application. If you don't meet the lender's minimum down payment requirement, you will not be able to proceed with your application until you've met that requirement.

INSIDER TIP:

Lenders do not pay much attention to household items being included in your net worth. When those items are listed, lenders know it's often due to the individual having a negative net worth or no net worth. Avoid listing household items as part of your net worth or viewing them as strong fallback positions. The same logic applies to life insurance policies. It's great for a lender to know you have life insurance, but a lender also wants to know how you will handle things if you get sick and do not die.

Also avoid listing the value of vehicles that are more than 10 years old. The value you assign to your car is probably subjective. Everyone believes their depreciating asset is worth more than its actual market value.

When a lender looks at your net worth, they are looking for liquid assets that can quickly be converted to cash. When you hold such assets in a large amount, you have a good fallback position.

COLLATERAL

When it comes to mortgage underwriting, collateral refers to the security of the home itself that is being financed. A mortgage loan is simply evidence of an interest in land that lenders take with the mortgage loan charge. The indication of such interest is registered on the title.

Even to well-qualified individuals, a lender might not extend a mortgage loan if the home they plan to put up for mortgage security purposes has adverse influences that make it less marketable for resale. The lender doesn't want a home beside a power station as most buyers might not find it as desirable to live beside a power station. A lender also might not want to secure a home with land next to train tracks because the location will be less desirable to potential buyers. Those are just some examples.

INSIDER TIP:

It's important to seek homes that are likely to appeal to most people so that prospective purchasers are good candidates to obtain financing in the bank's view. Most buyers do not have enough cash to buy a property outright; therefore, they will need to secure a mortgage loan in order to purchase a home.

That criteria doesn't mean you can't find something that's unique to you, but avoid finding something that only you will ever like as it might make it difficult for others who might desire your home to get financing.

Look at your potential property at different times in the day and take a drive around the area to identify any adverse influences. A lender might not catch all adverse influences, so don't assume because the lender approved the loan that they know all adverse influences about your property. Do an internet search on the property and call the city/town to find out any issues that might have been reported about the property or future development that might affect your property.

CAPACITY

Capacity looks at your ability to afford the mortgage loan you are seeking. A lender will confirm your income to determine if you can afford the monthly mortgage payments. Lenders also look at other expenses you are obligated to pay, such as property taxes, credit card balances, personal loans, strata or homeowner's association dues, and spousal support when determining your capacity.

Additionally, lenders have regulatory and insurer metrics that they also have to meet. For example, an insured mortgage will have a specific capacity ratio that the lender must ensure the borrower meets in order to qualify the loan for insurance. Each lender will also have their own capacity ratio as well. The two ratios used in mortgage application are known as total debt service ratio (TDS) and gross debt service (GDS). These ratios will be discussed in more detail in the coming chapters, but for now, just know that you will have to meet certain ratio criteria in order to show the lender you have capacity to afford the mortgage loan.

Similar to a lender's treatment of net worth considerations, not all employment income is viewed equally. For example, a long-tenure borrower will be viewed more favorably by a lender than someone who makes the same level of income but just started with the company. Law enforcement and professionals such as doctors or lawyers are looked at more favorably by lenders even if they might be on probation. Most law enforcement officers typically have a one-year probationary period, but during my time underwriting, lenders often waived their probationary guidelines for that line of work given their high job security and income level.

INSIDER TIP:

Before you apply for a mortgage, make sure you've completed your probationary period for most jobs. Anyone can be fired at any time, but during your probationary period, an employee is particularly susceptible to dismissal.

Some lenders will consider waiving your probationary period if you have several years of experience in the same industry or position. However, it's best to avoid applying for a mortgage when on probation to avoid any issues. Lastly, if you plan on changing jobs, do it after your mortgage has funded. You would not believe the number of mortgages that fail because the individual changes jobs after getting an approval but before funding. To make matters worse, they decide to only bring the job switch to light when they are signing with their lawyer and about to fund their mortgage. Don't make any major changes until your mortgage has funded.

CHAPTER 6

SAVE $10,000 WITH THE RIGHT TYPE OF MORTGAGE

Upon buying our first home, I noticed there was a large amount, just over $10,000, that was added to our mortgage loan. I didn't know what it was, but when I looked at the loan document, it said the amount was for a mortgage insurance premium. When I asked what the insurance was, I was told it was insurance we had to pay for since we didn't have at least a 20% down payment. I later discovered the type of mortgage loan we got was known as a high-ratio mortgage because we only had 5% of the purchase price as down payment, and anything less than 20% down required mortgage insurance.

There are two type of mortgages that can be obtained in Canada. You can have either a high-ratio mortgage or a conventional mortgage.[7]

THE HIGH-RATIO MORTGAGE

A high-ratio mortgage is a mortgage that has less than 20% down payment of the purchase price. Individuals who buy a home with a purchase price of less than $1 million and a down payment of less than 20% of the purchase price are required to obtain mortgage insurance through one of Canada's mortgage insurance providers.[8] In 2015, the Government of Canada made some changes regarding the minimum down payment required for an insured mortgage. The minimum was increased from 5% to 10% on the portion of the purchase price above $500,000. For example, if you wanted to purchase a home that was priced at $600,000, you would have to come up with a total down payment of $35,000 (0.05*500,000 plus 0.10*100,000), which came into effect as of February 15, 2016. The maximum purchase price of less than $1 million remained unchanged.[9]

There are three mortgage insurance providers in Canada: Canada Mortgage and Housing Corporation (CMHC), Sagen (previously Genworth Canada), and Canada Guaranty.[10] In 2020, Genworth Canada changed names after being bought by Brookfield Business Partners LP.[11]

---

7 "10 words to know when buying a home," CMHC, accessed August 12, 2021, https://www.cmhc-schl.gc.ca/en/professionals/industry-innovation-and-leadership/industry-expertise/resources-for-mortgage-professionals/10-words-to-know-when-buying-home.

8 "https://www.cmhc-schl.gc.ca/en/consumers/home-buying/mortgage-loan-insurance-for-consumers/what-is-mortgage-loan-insurance"

9 Canada, Department of Finance. "Government of Canada." Canada.ca, December 11, 2015. https://www.canada.ca/en/department-finance/news/2015/12/government-of-canada-takes-action-to-maintain-a-healthy-competitive-and-stable-housing-market.html.

10 "Mortgage Default Insurance (CMHC Insurance)," Ratehub, updated January 11, 2021, https://www.ratehub.ca/cmhc-mortgage-insurance.

11 Mark Rendell, "Brookfield to take full ownership of Genworth in $1.6-billion deal," The *Globe and Mail*, October 26, 2020, https://www.theglobeandmail.com/business/article-brookfield-to-take-full-ownership-of-mortgage-insurer-genworth-in-1/.

Lenders submit their mortgage loan applications to those three mortgage insurers for insurance approval.

Mortgage insurance is a simple concept in theory. A borrower who obtains a mortgage loan that requires mortgage insurance is required to pay a prescribed premium set by the mortgage insurer. The mortgage insurance premium paid by the borrower is placed into a pool, which the insurer uses to offset any losses the lender might suffer in the event of the borrower defaulting on the loan.

If someone is purchasing a home for $800,000 and only has 5% down payment, the lender is at a greater risk of a default loan than someone who has a 35% down payment. Lenders are not willing to take on such a risk given the overall potential exposure to default on such a loan. In that the ability of many people to get mortgage loans would be difficult, the government, wanting to encourage homeownership, devised a means to make lenders feel more comfortable by giving them greater loan security through mortgage insurance. In essence, the lender is made whole if the borrower defaults on a mortgage loan that has been insured.

Mortgage insurance is for the lender, not the borrower, but the borrower pays the premium on behalf of the lender. The borrower can pay the premium in two ways: roll the premium fees into their mortgage loan, or they can pay it out directly to the lender to forward the payment directly to the insurer.

Lenders tend to offer their best rates on high-ratio mortgage due to the low risk of such loans. It might feel unfair to have the borrower pay the premium and not get any protection for paying that fee; however, the reality is that no one would lend someone 95% of an $800,000 loan without a sure way to get the money back. You too would likely feel much better having to only give someone 50% of the money rather than 95% to reduce the amount you might lose if they don't pay you back.

When it comes to the types of insured mortgages available, they fall into three buckets: insured, insurable, and uninsurable.

An insured mortgage loan is one that qualifies for mortgage insurance with the borrower paying the associated mortgage premium.

An insurable mortgage loan is one that meets the insurer's guidelines, but the borrower is not required to obtain mortgage insurance. The term insurable means the lender can look to pay for insurance to have the loan insured.[12] For example, a borrower who has 25% down payment of the purchase price isn't required to get mortgage insurance. However, the lender may still want to insure the loan, perhaps to make the loan more marketable to securitize (i.e., sell the loan to another bank or an investor). In this case, the lender could insure the loan and would pay the associated premium itself, which usually is factored into the loan rate charged by the lender. That option is referred to as back-end insuring. It doesn't happen often and most of the big banks do not do it. However, some monoline lenders (lenders that only lend mortgages) may do it to make the loan more enticing for investors.

The opposite of an insured loan is one that is uninsurable, either because it doesn't qualify for mortgage insurance or it doesn't meet the insurer's guidelines.

THE CONVENTIONAL MORTGAGE

The opposite of a high-ratio mortgage is a conventional mortgage, which is one where an individual has at least 20% or more of the down payment on the purchase price and is not required to obtain mortgage insurance.

---

12 Canada, Financial Consumer Agency of. "Government of Canada." Canada.ca, June 28, 2021. https://www.canada.ca/en/financial-consumer-agency/services/mortgages/down-payment. html#toc1.

Conventional mortgage lending limits are based on the lender's guidelines. In theory, there is no limit, but lenders do have limits on how much they will lend a borrower. The purchase price of homes for conventional mortgages isn't set at the less than one-million-dollar limit as with high-ratio mortgages. Additionally, conventional mortgages can have a longer amortization term compared to high-ratio mortgage. For example, at the time of this writing, the maximum amortization for an insured mortgage is 25 years;[13] the maximum amortization for a conventional mortgage is 30 years.[14]

When starting your mortgage journey, you will likely be getting an insured mortgage and then move to a conventional mortgage loan.

---

13 "Mortgage Default Insurance (CMHC Insurance)."

14 Tim Bennett, "Can I get a 30-year mortgage in Canada?" Ratehub, August 17, 2020, https:// www.ratehub.ca/blog/can-i-get-a-30-year-mortgage-in-canada/.

CHAPTER 7

YOU CAN DO 100% FINANCED HOMES

(PLUS OTHER PROGRAMS YOU MAY NOT KNOW ABOUT)

When I started my role as an underwriter, I was amazed to find out that lenders have a host of insurance programs they can access to reduce their loan risk. The home we purchased had an unfinished basement, which we planned to renovate in order to rent it out. I wish I knew some of this information when we bought our house as we could have utilized some of these insurance programs, such as the purchase plus improvement program offered by insurers.[15] But since I didn't find out about these programs until after I started the underwriting role,

---

15 "CMHC Improvement." CMHC. Accessed September 14, 2021. https://www.cmhc-schl. gc.ca/en/professionals/project-funding-and-mortgage-financing/mortgage-loan-insurance/ mortgage-loan-insurance-homeownership-programs/cmhc-improvement.

which was a few years after we bought our house, we financed the renovation ourselves.

While there are three insurers in Canada, the bulk of the insurance business is dominated by two providers: CMHC and Sagen. These two insurers are most often used by lenders when obtaining mortgage insurance coverage.

The insurance programs offered to lenders by these insurers are similar among all three insurers. Lenders find these programs extremely beneficial as it reduces their loan risk exposure. But they also benefit homeowners as they enable them to purchase a home with smaller required down payment.

The insurers have several insurance programs that lenders can utilize to help them meet the needs of a variety of potential borrowers. Each program's qualification is slightly different, but in general the programs require a minimum credit score of 600,[16] at least 5% down payment of the purchase price, purchase price less than $1 million, and gross debt service (GDS) and total debt service ratio (TDS) of 32:42.

Some insurers will also consider a GDS/TDS ratio up to 39:44 if the borrower has a strong credit profile. There have been changes recently to prevent borrowers owning multiple properties that are insured, which means you can only have one property insured at any one time, and refinanced mortgages no longer qualify for mortgage insurance.

I will provide a high-level overview of the some of the insurer's programs available to lenders. My intention is just to give you a general insight into what kind of programs a lender might be using in qualifying you for a mortgage loan. The program overview I provide is based on my past

16 "Mortgage Loan Insurance: Benefits and Requirements." CMHC. Accessed September 14, 2021. https://www.cmhc-schl.gc.ca/en/professionals/project-funding-and-mortgage-financing/mortgage-loan-insurance/mortgage-loan-insurance-homeownership-programs/mortgage-loan-insurance-quick-reference-guide.

underwriting experience along with information found on CMHC's and Sagen's websites. You can find more details on CMHC's specific programs at www.cmhc.ca and Sagen's programs at www.sagen.ca.

STANDARD 5% DOWN PROGRAM

This program allows lenders to qualify a potential homebuyer for mortgage insurance with as little as 5% down payment of the purchase price. It is the most common program used by all lenders for first-time homebuyers. It's a popular program among lenders and borrowers.

PURCHASE PLUS IMPROVEMENT

This program is designed to help lenders insure loans for borrowers who plan on doing some renovation after taking possession.[17] It's another popular program because it allows borrowers to add the renovation cost after it's been completed to their mortgage. For example, a buyer who has $20,000 toward a renovation purchases a home with a dated kitchen and plans to redo the kitchen with the $20,000. Normally, the individual would purchase the home and then proceed to complete the renovation with their savings upon taking possession. However, with this program, they can work with their lender to do a purchase plus improvement mortgage. In doing so, the lender can insure the loan based on the total expected value after the renovation.

Let's assume the home was purchased at $400,000 with 5% down. After renovation of the kitchen, the expected market value works out to be $420,000. The buyer would put down 5% of the expected after-renovation value, which is $21,000. They would be qualified for a $420,000 loan amount instead of the initial $400,000 purchase price. At

---

17   https://www.cmhc-schl.gc.ca/en/professionals/project-funding-and-mortgage-financing/ mortgage-loan-insurance/mortgage-loan-insurance-homeownership-programs/cmhc-improvement

the time of funding, the lender would hold back $20,000, which is the cost of the kitchen renovation, and fund the rest of the mortgage loan. The buyer would move into their home and commence construction of the kitchen. Once the kitchen has been confirmed to be completed, the bank would release the remaining $20,000 to the buyer and increase the mortgage to 95% of the $420,000 post-renovation value.

That option is advantageous to the homebuyer as they will be able to recoup most of the renovation cost by being able to add it to their original mortgage loan. Therefore, they don't permanently lose the cash they had saved up and can have it available as an emergency fund.

While there are positives to the program, in my experience it is difficult for first-time homebuyers if they lack access to credit or don't have the savings required to complete the renovation on hand. To carry out the program, you have to have access to the funds required to complete the renovation, which most first-time purchasers likely do not have as they are simply trying to get into the market. Second, most first-time homebuyers use credit cards to complete their renovations, and their renovation doesn't always have a 1:1 return. For example, the kitchen renovation might initially be quoted as costing $20,000 but ends up costing $25,000. The bank isn't going to lend you more money unless the post-renovation market value can support $425,000 value and you qualify for that loan amount. Third, most homeowners tend to complete renovations that add to the esthetic of the home rather than adding to the value of the home. The insurers do check the type of renovations to avoid that situation, but sometimes renovations are accepted that really add no value to the home.

The key with this program is to first have access to the renovation funds. Then, do proper research on your renovation to ensure it will not have an excessive cost overrun (most recommend adding 10% to the estimate because all renovations incur additional costs). And lastly, complete renovations that add value to a home. Typically, renovations that add value to homes are bedroom additions, suite additions, and kitchen/bathroom updates.

NEW TO CANADA PROGRAM

This program allows lenders to qualify recent immigrants to purchase a home with as little as 5% down. When at the bank where I worked, Sagen's programs required the borrower to have minimum full-time employment in Canada for at least 3 months[18] and to have immigrated or relocated to Canada within the last 60 months. The CMHC Newcomers program is available to both permanent and non-permanent residents, but the latter must be legally authorized to work in Canada.[19]

SELF-EMPLOYED PROGRAM

This program is designed to allow lenders to insure a mortgage loan to individuals who are self-employed.[20] The program is similar to the standard 5% program, except it's meant for self-employed borrowers. Most self-employed individuals have difficulty qualifying for a loan because often their reported net income on their tax returns is not a true reflection of their income. Self-employed owners can write off expenses, which often reduces the amount of income they claim. While that rule results in them paying lower taxes, it also results in their struggling to qualify for mortgages as their confirmed income is lower than what they actually made.

---

18   "New to Canada Program," Sagen, accessed August 12, 2021, https://www.sagen.ca/products-and-services/new-to-canada/.

19   "Mortgage Loan Insurance: CMHC Newcomers," CMHC, accessed August 12, 2021, https://assets.cmhc-schl.gc.ca/sf/project/cmhc/pdfs/factsheets/new/cmhc-newcomers-fact-sheet.pdf?rev=f65a751b-b70a-4e0c-a9b1-5b2a48b1658a.

20   "Mortgage Loan Insurance: CMHC Self-Employed," CMHC, accessed August 12, 2021, https://assets.cmhc-schl.gc.ca/sf/project/cmhc/pdfs/factsheets/new/cmhc-self-employed-fact-sheet.pdf?rev=4a7139cb-a613-44bb-80df-b4ce64ef98e8.

The program is designed to help with that problem by providing some options to self-employed borrowers by allowing them to "gross up" their net business income. It's important to note that the program is not a "no income required" program. You still need an income and must be able to show at least two years of that income level. A self-employed individual will be qualified the same way as an employed person, but lenders calculate self-employed income differently to account for their ability to write off their expenses. Typically, they allow a self-employed individual's income to be grossed up by a certain percentage.

INVESTMENT PROPERTY

This program allows a lender to place insurance on an investment mortgage loan. Two major qualifying criteria for this program are a minimum down payment of 20% of the purchase price and the purchase has to be less than $1 million.[21] Lastly, this program requires the investment property purchase to be at least two units.

BORROWED DOWN PAYMENT

Most people will be surprised to know you can technically do 100% financing in Canada. This program allows a lender to place insurance on a mortgage loan when the down payment came from a borrowed source.[22] For example, let's assume you would like to purchase a home for $400,000. The minimum down payment required is 5%, which amounts to $20,000. If you do not have $20,000 saved up (cash) but you do have a line of credit or credit card in that amount, you can qualify for

21 "Mortgage Loan Insurance: CHMC Income Property," CMHC, accessed August 12, 2021, https://assets.cmhc-schl.gc.ca/sf/project/cmhc/pdfs/factsheets/new/cmhc-income-property-fact-sheet.pdf?rev=ba301ebf-e074-489f-8c40-f6b3f04248da.

22 "Borrowed Down Payment," Sagen online, accessed November 22, 2021, https://www.sagen.ca/products-and-services/borrowed-down-payment/.

the mortgage amount by using the line of credit or credit card as your down payment.

The lender can obtain mortgage insurance for that loan to protect themselves. In essence, the loan becomes 100% financed. The mortgage premium rates charged by insurers for that type of coverage is higher as borrowed down payments are considered non-traditional sources. While the program is available, its actual usage is limited and the standard 5% down program is no longer eligible under Sagan's borrowed down program and CMHC.[23] However, purchase plus improvement and vacation/secondary homes are still eligible for this program.[24]

VACATION OR SECOND HOME PROGRAM

This program allows a lender to qualify a vacation or second home for insurance with as little as 5% down payment.[25] Eligible properties under this program include seasonal properties and year-round winterized properties.

FAMILY PLAN

This program allows a lender to place insurance on a mortgage loan offered to an individual who helps another family member purchase a home but will not be residing in the property.[26] One example is a parent who co-signs for a mortgage with their child for a home but will not

---

23 Alexandra MacQueen, "CMCH Tightens Mortgage Rules in Latest Response to COVID-19," Money Sense online, June 8, 2020, https://www.moneysense.ca/spend/real-estate/cmhc-tightens-mortgage-rules-in-latest-response-to-covid-19/.

24 "Borrowed Down Payment," Sagen online.

25 "Vacation/Secondary Homes," Sagan online, accessed November 16, 2021, https://www.sagen.ca/products-and-services/vacation-secondary-homes/.

26 "Family Plan Program," Sagan online, accessed November 16, 2021, https://www.sagen.ca/products-and-services/family-plan/.

reside there. The program requires that all family members be on the title, even though they do not plan to reside at the property.

Those are just some of the programs that lenders can utilize to get additional security for their loan by insuring the mortgage loan. They are not the only programs available, but they are the major ones. Please refer to your lender or individual you are working with for up-to-date information as such programs often change or might be discontinued by the time you read this book.

CHAPTER 8

DO YOU KNOW YOUR BNI SCORE?

applied for my first credit card when I was a student and was declined. I didn't understand why, as I was working and didn't have any debt. It turns out that even though I was working, I was declined because I had no established credit and was trying to apply for a regular credit card. I went to another bank, and the advisor explained to me that I first have to get a student credit card to establish my credit as the lending guideline is different than those qualifications for a regular credit card. That was my first experience with credit. Since I worked at the bank when we applied for our first mortgage, I had a decent understanding of credit score as I often submitted credit applications for clients. I knew that when applying for a loan you usually have to hit a certain credit score number. For example, at the time of our mortgage application, the minimum mortgage credit score requirement was 600.

Credit is one of the 5 C's a lender will consider when determining if you will qualify for a mortgage loan. Most of the information a lender will rely on for your credit profile will come from your credit report. Some lenders have a minimum credit score in order to be approved for a mortgage loan. In addition to a credit score requirement set by the lender, mortgage insurers also have their own credit scores that borrowers must meet to qualify for an insurance program.

But what exactly is a credit score? A credit score is a three-digit number assigned to an individual and is designed to help predict the financial delinquency of an individual. The number ranges from 300 to 900— the higher the number, the better the credit score.[27] In my experience, the credit score number is not scientific as it doesn't always tell the full story of someone's credit history. There are two major companies that lenders in Canada use to obtain a borrower's credit score: TransUnion and Equifax.[28] Most of the lenders will use Equifax and have TransUnion as a backup, although toward the end of my time in underwriting, TransUnion was being pulled in addition to Equifax.

Your credit score number is determined based on five factors:

- ⊕ Your payment history
- ⊕ Your credit utilization (credit used vs. your available credit)
- ⊕ The length of credit history
- ⊕ Public records
- ⊕ Number of inquiries into your credit file

Each category has a weight assigned to it, and typically the breakdown of each category is:

- ⊕ 35% toward your payment history

---

27 "What is a Good Credit Score?" Equifax, accessed August 12, 2021, https://www.consumer.equifax.ca/personal/education/credit-score/what-is-a-good-credit-score/.

28 Canada, Financial Consumer Agency of. "Government of Canada." Canada.ca, May 13, 2020. https://www.canada.ca/en/financial-consumer-agency/services/credit-reports-score/credit-report-score-basics.html.

- → 30% toward your credit utilization
- → 15% toward your credit history
- → 10% toward public records
- → 10% toward inquiries

As you can see, the bulk of your credit score is based on your payment history, credit utilization, and credit history.[29] People are often concerned about too many inquiries when shopping around for a mortgage, but the reality is it has less of an impact on your overall credit score than it's believed to. You shouldn't be afraid to shop around when seeking a mortgage loan; however, avoid looking excessively as eventually the inquiries will impact your credit score.

If you do shop around, let each lender know that you've been shopping around when submitting your application and which lenders you've applied to along with why you didn't go with them. Lenders are okay with your shopping around as long as you let them know during your initial submission.

REPAIR BEFORE APPLYING

If you have a poor credit score and are looking to improve it before you apply for a mortgage, here's where you should focus your effort.

First, ensure your payment history is good. Always ensure you've paid the minimum balance that's due each month. Lenders want to see that you can honor your commitment. A poor repayment history lets a lender know you tend to not keep your word. If you're behind on payments, take baby steps and start with paying the minimum payment owed and work your way to eventually paying more than the minimum payment. Payment history is what's important, and even if the minimum payments don't pay

---

29 "What is a Good Credit Score?" similar to 22

off the debt, they at least will keep your credit history clean and improve your credit score.

Next, look at your credit utilization as it's something most people do not understand. It's often the second biggest reason that people have a low credit score in my experience. Here's an example: Let's assume you have a credit card with a limit of $1,000. Each month, you use the credit card to pay for all your expenses to earn some points and pay off the balance in full. Let's assume the total expenses charged to your card comes to $800 per month. Thus, each month, you charge $800 and pay off your credit card in full when the statement comes due.

In that example, your credit utilization is 80% (800/1000*100). Said differently, you use 80% of the available credit you have every single month. Despite paying off the entire balance in full each month, your credit score will be impacted negatively. Why? Since you are using almost all the available credit you have access to, you are at a higher risk of being delinquent. The ding to your credit history might seem odd, but from a risk standpoint it makes sense. If you use almost all your credit every month, then all it takes is a job loss or something bad to occur and you will be unable to make the payment in full as you've been doing.

One possible solution to this problem might also seem odd. You need to increase your credit limit. When you increase your credit limit, you will in effect reduce your credit utilization, which will reflect positively in your credit score. A general rule is to keep your credit utilization below 30%. The other solution is to pay for more items in cash and use your credit card in a manner that keeps your credit utilization below 30%.

The next three items—credit history, public records, and inquiries—round up the rest of your credit score. For credit history, avoid closing credit cards with which you've had a long history and get a variety of credit products from loans to credit cards. Public records are items such as judgment, bankruptcy, consumer proposal, or collections that are reported on your credit report. Lenders are more likely to decline an applicant who's had a bankruptcy that was a result of a previous real estate purchase or foreclosure. If you get an approval with such a history, that risk will be priced into your rate, or the lender may request an additional amount of down payment.

The key to having a good credit score is to stay focused on making payments on time and in full while ensuring your credit utilization is low. If you do both, you will be able to have a credit score sufficient to meet most lenders' minimum score requirement. Finally, there's another lesser known credit tool—the Bankruptcy Navigator Index (BNI)—which lenders use for mortgage applications. The BNI score predicts the likelihood of bankruptcy within 24 months. Scores range from 1-999. The higher your score, the less likely you are to experience bankruptcy. Some of the factors that drives your BNI score are:

- ➔ Credit utilization
- ➔ Payment history
- ➔ Public records or prior bankruptcy
- ➔ Past payment history
- ➔ Length of history

The Bankruptcy Navigator Index (BNI) score is designed to catch individuals who use credit to pay off credit.[30] It's possible for someone to have a great credit score if they simply move credit around each month by transferring balances from one card to another. The BNI score tries to capture these individuals. Similar to the credit score, it's more of an art than a science. Some lenders have strict requirements for BNI while others use it less in their underwriter process or might not at all.

---

30 "Bankruptcy Navigator Index 5.0," Equifax, accessed August 12, 2021, https://www.equifax.com/business/bankruptcy-navigator-index/.

In short, you want to have a high credit and BNI score. A high credit score tells a lender that you honor your debt commitments and understand how to use credit. A high BNI score tells a lender that you pay your bills off each month and are not "robbing Peter to pay Paul." The best way to ensure a good credit and BNI score is to take on only commitments you can afford and pay your bills off each month in full. Some things in life don't need to be complicated.

CHAPTER 9

UNCOVERING A GREAT CREDIT SCORE

Now that you understand how your credit report works, you should order your personal credit report to review its details. Credit reports can seem intimidating at first, but you don't need to fear them. A credit report is no harder to read than a report card once you know the code.

I recall when I got my first credit report. I had no clue how to read it. I ordered the free copy of my report, and back then I didn't even see the credit score on that report. I felt as though I was reading a report that I didn't fully know how to make sense of. This chapter will help you better understand what you will be looking at.

You can obtain your credit report today much more easily than in the past. Previously, you had to mail in your request to one of the major credit agencies to obtain your free credit report. Today, some banks offer built-in credit reports through online banking, which will give you all the details you will need, including your credit score. If your bank doesn't offer the feature, I strongly recommend you purchase your personal credit report to review on your own before you start your mortgage application. You can purchase your credit report directly from Equifax or TransUnion online. Both still offer free ones, but I find those to be limited and feel it's worth paying to get the same report the lenders are getting about you.

To assist you in reading your report, let's go over each section to help you understand.

PERSONAL DETAILS

Personal details include your name, address, social insurance number, and employment. Ensure your credit report is accurate regarding each of those details, especially your name and social insurance number. It's also important to check that your address and employment is accurate. In my experience, those details tend to not be accurate. Don't worry if your old address is still showing as you might not have applied for any credit since a recent move, which might be the reason your address or employment details haven't been updated. Lenders will not hold anything against you if the address on the credit report doesn't match your current one, but come prepared to supply five years of your address history.

PUBLIC RECORDS

Public records are details publicly available that show up on your credit report. They include bankruptcy, collections, family support records, and judgments, to name a few. In this section, you want to ensure you don't have derogatory public records on your report, unless they are warranted.

If you've gone through a bankruptcy, ensure you've completed it and have your proof of completion available to provide to the lender. If anything appears in this section that you are not aware of or that is untrue, you'll want to investigate and correct the information before applying for your mortgage. You'd be surprised at what shows up on a credit report that should not have been attributed to you.

TRADE DETAILS

Trades are the current debts and obligations you have on your credit report. Check to ensure the trade information reporting on your credit report is accurate. Ensure all the credit details on your report are actually the credit or loans you have. Go through all the trades and check for accuracy. For credit cards, check that the credit limits are correct. For installment loans, such as car loan, ensure the initial loan amount and monthly payment are correct. For current or prior mortgages, ensure the lender and monthly payment are correct. Some mortgage lenders do not report to the credit bureau. I've found most lenders that do not report on your credit report tend to be private lenders. Monoline lenders (companies that only do mortgage loans) usually do not report to the credit bureau under their public operating name. They are usually registered under another legal name or company, which reports to the credit bureau. If you already have or had a mortgage, ensure it shows up with the **M** code in the details section of your credit score (see chart that follows). If it's not reported, you will not get credit for your payment history.

Next, ensure all your credit trades are reported as the specific letter and number for the corresponding trade. For example, your car loan should report as the letter I with the number 1 after it. You want to see a 1 after the letter for any other trade that shows up. An I1 trade means you are up to date and have paid as agreed. If you do not see R1 (revolving credit) or I1 (installment loan), then you need to bring those accounts up to date as they are past due. You will have to wait a few months for the credit agency report to reflect the correction.

The Financial Consumer Agency of Canada has a great chart, which I've included here with their permission, that really explains credit report letters and their meaning, as shown in the chart below.[31]

WHAT LETTERS MEAN IN A RATING ON A CREDIT REPORT		
Letter	**Meaning**	**Example**
I	Install Credit-You borrow money for a specific period of time. You make regular payments in fixed amounts until you pay off the loan.	Car Loan
O	Open Status Credit-You may borrow money when you need to, up to a certain limit.	Mobile Phone Account
R	Revolving or Recurring Credit-You may borrow money up to your credit limit on an ongoing basis. You make regular payments in varying amounts depending on the balance of your account.	Credit Card
M	Mortgage Loan-Mortgage information may be included on your credit report.	Mortgage

Number	Meaning
0	• Too new to rate • Approved, but not yet used
1	• Paid within 30 days of billing • Pays as agreed
2	Late payment: 31 to 59 days late
3	Late payment: 60 to 89 days late
4	Late payment: 90 to 119 days late

31 "Understanding your credit report," Government of Canada, accessed August 12, 2021, https://www.canada.ca/en/financial-consumer-agency/services/credit-reports-score/understand-credit-report.html.

5	Late payment: more than 120 days late, but not yet rated "9"
6	This code isn't used
7	Making regular payments using one of the following debt management options: • a consolidation order • orderly payment of debts • consumer proposal • debt management program with a credit counselling agency
8	Repossession
9	• Written off as a "bad debt" • Sent to collection agency • Bankruptcy

INQUIRY DETAILS

For this section, simply make sure the inquiries you see were made by you. If you see a credit inquiry from a lender you did not apply or believe wasn't by you, investigate it further by reaching out to the lender or financial institution shown. If the inquiry details look good, then move on from this section.

That's it for how to read your credit report. After reading the last two chapters, you should know how your credit score is determined and how to read your own credit report. I recommend that you pull your credit report at least once every year. That practice will help you know where your credit stands and offer the chance to catch any potential fraud.

It's worth repeating: The best way to have a great credit score is to pay off all your debts in full each month, keep your credit utilization low, and only take on debt that you can afford.

CHAPTER 10

NOT ALL INCOME IS EQUAL TO BANKS

The first mortgage application for our home was initially declined due to our not meeting the lender's TDS ratio, but we also had some challenges with my income. At the time of our application, I had moved from the advisor role to a credit analyst role for auto underwriting. Since I had just changed jobs and most banks have a six-month probationary period at the time, I was still under probation at the time of our mortgage application.

While the second lender approved our mortgage application, they did so on the condition that I had to have completed my probationary period. As a result of that condition, I had to call our realtor back and ask for our closing date to be pushed back in order to be able to provide a letter to the lender confirming I was no longer on probation. I hadn't anticipated my change of jobs to be a problem because I was still in the banking sector and especially since my salary had actually increased, so I was surprised to see the conditional approval. But the real stress was knowing

I could be fired in the meantime and then be sued by the seller for us not closing on the home we had just accepted to purchase. It all worked out in the end, but you should be aware of the type of income lenders often see and a general idea of what they expect from you. The chart that follows here will outline some common incomes most people have or use for their mortgage application. I've provided some details on the type of documentation that lenders might request for each source of income along with some additional comments you should be aware of depending on the income type.

Please keep in mind, similar to mortgage rules, income requirement does change frequently. Therefore, don't use this as reference guide but rather as a tool to inform yourself as to the general type of income a lender might accept and what type of documentation they might request. To get the most up to date accepted income and documentation required, you should speak directly with your lender or professional you are working with for your mortgage.

EMPLOYMENT TYPE	EMPLOYMENT REQUIREMENT	DOCUMENTATION REQUIRED
Permanent Full-Time or Part-Time	• Probationary period is over. • No minimum length of employment is normally required.	• Recent current paystub within 30 days of funding date. • Current letter from employer (confirming position, salary, and start date). *Note: Lender might also complete verbal confirmation with employer.*

Casual, Seasonal, Contract	• Minimum 24 months of employment history with the same employer. • Some lenders may accept 24 months of same industry work with different employers.	• Recent paystub within 30 days of the funding date. • Letter from employer (confirming position, salary, and start date). *Note: Lenders want to see two years of history with the same employer; additional documentation might be requested if they have concern around the sustainability of the income being claimed.*
Overtime, Tips, Bonus, or Commission	• Minimum 24 months of income history with same employer. • Current year-to-date paystub must be on track to meet the 24 months' equivalent income that you wish to use.	• Recent paystub within 30 days of funding date. • Most recent two years of T4* statements from employer. *Note: If T4 from your most recent year shows decreasing income, the lender is likely to not do a two-year average.*
Paid Maternity or Paid Parental Leave	• Confirmation from employer confirming maternity leave or parental leave. • Lender will use either full normal income level or might exclude a certain percentage of the income depending on area.	• Letter of employment from employer (confirming normal employment details, confirming maternity leave, expected return date, and salary upon return). *Note: Lender might request additional documents if they have concern about sustainability of income level.*

Self-Employment Income	• Minimum of 24 months of operating the business. • Income calculated based on two-year average. • Income can be grossed up by a certain percentage.	• Most recent two years of T1*. • Most recent two years of notice of assessment (NOA).
Investment Income	• Investment holdings must show ability to sustain income through the term of the mortgage loan.	• Most recent investment statements. • Recent bank statements showing investment income deposit. *Note: Lender might also ask for T1 or tax documents to confirm you've actually been receiving income from your investment and claiming the income.*
Pension Income	• Pension statement confirming amount being received.	• Most recent bank statement showing pension deposit. • Most recent T4A*, T4A (P)*, T4A (OAS)* statement.
Child/ Spousal Support Payments	• Agreement confirming payment to be received.	• Most recent bank statement showing 6-24 months of payment history. • Court order or written separation agreement witnessed by lawyer or notary. *Note: Lenders want to see these payments being received consistently each month. Some may not accept the source of income if it isn't consistent.*

| Rental Income | • Agreement confirming amount of rent being received.
 • Some lenders will hire an appraisal to provide a comparable market rent assessment if rental is new or have questions about the rental agreement. | • Current signed rental agreement.
 • Most recent bank statement confirming rental deposit.
 • Statement of Real Estate Rentals (T776*).

 Note: Lenders may request confirmation of bank deposit history from 1-12 months. |

* T4: Summary statement (slip) of your employment earnings and deductions for the year.[32]

* T1: General Income Tax and Benefit Return that summarizes the taxpayer's income, deductions, and tax payable.[33]

* T4A: Statement confirming pension, retirement, annuity, and other income.[34]

* T4A (P): Statement confirming Canada Pension Plan benefit.[35]

* T4A (OAS): Statement confirming Old Age Security benefit.[36]

* T776: Form used to declare income and expense related to income earned from renting real estate or other real property. [37]

---

32 "What is a T4 slip?" Government of Canada, accessed August 13, 2021, https://www.canada.ca/en/revenue-agency/services/tax/individuals/educational-programs/learning-about-taxes/learning-material/module-4-completing-a-simple-tax-return/your-t4-information-slip.html.

33 "What is a T1 General Income Tax and Benefit Return?" H&R Block, accessed August 13, 2021, https://www.hrblock.ca/taxform/what-is-a-t1-general-income-tax-and-benefit-return/.

34 "What is the difference between a T4A, T4A(P) and a T4A (OAS) slip?" H&R Block, accessed August 13, 2021, https://help.hrblockonline.ca/hc/en-ca/articles/115002464228-What-s-the-difference-between-a-T4A-T4A-P-and-a-T4A-OAS-slip/.

35 Ibid.

36 Ibid.

37 "Completing Form T776, Statement of Real Estate Rentals," Government of Canada, accessed August 13, 2021, https://www.canada.ca/en/revenue-agency/services/tax/businesses/topics/rental-income/completing-form-t776-statement-real-estate-rentals.html.

CHAPTER 11

THE DEBT BANKS LOOK AT

ncome is only one side of the equation when it comes to qualifying for your mortgage. A lender will also need to get an account of your debts to determine what you can actually afford. This section explains the type of payment used by lenders based on the debt. The chart will help you understand what amount of payment the lender is including for your debt obligations.

DEBT TYPE	PAYMENT AMOUNT USED	GENERAL COMMENTS
Credit Card(s)[38]	• 3% of the balance outstanding.	• Lenders will require a higher amount if upon pulling your credit report, it shows a higher minimum credit card payment than the 3% of the outstanding balance.

---

38 "What are the Different Kinds of Debt?" Equifax online, accessed November 16, 2021, https://www.equifax.com/personal/education/covid-19/types-of-consumer-debts/.

Unsecured Line(s) of Credit	• 3% of the balance outstanding.	• Some lenders will take the full available limit even if you haven't utilized the balance.
Installment Loan(s)	• Full monthly payment amount.	
Equity Line(s) of Credit	• Payment usually based on current 5-year fixed rate amortized over 25 years.	• Some lenders will use the entire equity line of credit limit approved. • Some lenders will calculate the amount based on the current balance outstanding.
Spousal Support Payments	• Full court order amount required.	
Child Support Payments	• Full court order amount required.	
Cell Phone	• None.	• Lenders normally do not include an amount but will require account be brought up to date if balance is owed or account is in arrears.
Outstanding Collections	• None.	• Amounts not used, but lenders will require collection be paid in full and account be brought up to date before mortgage funding.

Judgments	• None.	• No amount, but lenders will require judgment to be removed before proceeding with mortgage funding. • Depending on the type or reason for judgment, lenders might decline the application.
Mortgage(s)	• Full monthly payment amount.	• See calculations at end of chart.
Heating Costs	• Varies.	• Lenders typically use a formula to determine heating cost based on square footage and age of the home.
Condominium/ Strata Fees/ Homeowner Association (HOA) Dues	• 50% of the monthly fee.	• Some lenders take full HOA amount.
Rent(s)	• Full monthly rent amount.	• If you share rent, expect the lender to take the full rent amount, not just your portion of the rent
Rental Properties	• Full amount of the mortgage payment.	• Some lenders will omit heating cost for rental property if confirmed paid by tenant
Property Taxes	• Full annualized tax amount.	• Some lenders take net property taxes after any credit you might be entitled to. • Some lenders do not take tax credit into consideration.

MORTGAGE PAYMENT CALCULATION

One important thing to know is how lenders calculate the mortgage payment amount used for your initial application. To do so, lenders typically take the current mortgage rate, loan amount, amortization, and term to determine your mortgage payment.

For example, let's assume you want a five-year fixed-rate mortgage with a 25-year amortization. The current five-year fixed rate is 2%, and the mortgage amount you are seeking is $300,000. The lender would calculate your mortgage payment by taking the 2% rate on the $300,000 loan and amortize it over 25 years. For this example, the mortgage payment will work out to be a monthly payment of $1,270.35. Most mortgages in Canada are partially amortized, which means the payment is based on the number of amortization years even though you are only guaranteed your mortgage rate for the term you've signed up for. Once the term is up, you will either renew for another term or pay out the full loan balance to the lender.

Now, what I am about to explain is somewhat technical, but it is important to be aware of recent changes that the government has made regarding mortgage qualification. Your lender or the professional you are working with to secure your mortgage should be able to explain it to you in greater detail, assuming the rules haven't changed again in between.

In 2010, the Canadian government made some changes in how individuals qualify for mortgages.[39] If individuals were seeking a mortgage term under five years or a variable rate mortgage, the individual would first have to qualify for the mortgage loan amount at the Bank of Canada benchmark rate. For example, let's assume you're applying for a loan for $300,000 and the Bank of Canada benchmark rate was 4.74% (hypothetical rate). If you wanted to take a five-year variable rate

---

39   link to source- https://www.cbc.ca/news/business/mortgages-changing-the-rules-1.890956

mortgage that was at 3%, you would first need to show you could qualify for the mortgage loan at the Bank of Canada benchmark rate of 4.74%. As such, the monthly mortgage payment the lender will use is $1,700.68 rather than $1,419.74, which is the payment you will get at 3% based on a 25-year amortization. If you qualify at the Bank of Canada benchmark rate, then you will be able to get the lower rate at 3%. However, if you could not qualify at the higher rate, then you would have to see if you could qualify at the current five-year fixed rate at the time, which would have been higher than the variable rate but likely lower than the Bank of Canada benchmark rate.

Fast forward to today, and you might have heard people talking recently about changes to mortgage qualification known as B20 or the stress test.[40] Essentially, what the government did was apply the 2010 rule to all types of mortgages with one other addition. Individuals applying for a mortgage loan as of 2018 in Canada would have to qualify at the greater rate between the qualifying contract rate plus 2% or the Bank of Canada benchmark rate. Using our previous example, it would mean you would actually have to qualify at 5% (3% variable rate + 2%) instead of the Bank of Canada benchmark rate of 4.74%. The new rules were designed to protect Canadians and the real estate industry by ensuring mortgage borrowers could support mortgage payments at higher interest rates. The rules are still in place in an effort to avoid the market overheating.[41] However, given the current low interest rate environment, it appears the rule isn't having the effect the government intended. As such, when applying for a mortgage today in 2022 you have to qualify at a higher rate than your actual contract rate, which is what is being referred to as the stress test. The requirement applies to both high-ratio mortgages as well as conventional mortgages, regardless of the term or amortization selected.

---

40 Nicholas Saminather, "Canada proposes tighter mortgage stress test as home prices surge," Reuters, April 8, 2021, https://www.reuters.com/article/us-canada-mortgages-regulation/canada-proposes-tighter-mortgage-stress-test-as-home-prices-surge-idUSKBN2BV2NK.

41 Ibid.

CHAPTER 12

THE TWO-PARTY APPROVAL SYSTEM

Two ratios are important to know when it comes to mortgage financing. The first is gross debt service ratio (GDS). The second is total debt service ratio (TDS).

As I mentioned in the previous chapters, our first mortgage application was declined due to our total debt service (TDS) not being within the first lender's guideline. At the time, I didn't really get an explanation as to what TDS was and how it was calculated. I felt frustrated because I was being told they couldn't approve us but wasn't provided the insight into what exactly was the reason.

When the other lender approved us, I was really puzzled. When I entered the underwriting role, I realized what had happened in our application. I discovered since we got a high-ratio mortgage, it took two parties to approve us. The first was our lender and the second the insurer. The first lender we submitted our application to wasn't comfortable with our

TDS ratio. As such, we didn't meet their guideline, and therefore, our application wasn't even sent to the insurer for review. The second lender was willing to stretch our TDS to the max allowed, which was 44%, and forwarded our application to the insurer for approval to get additional guarantee for the loan. When they got the approval from the insurer, the second lender was more than willing to approve the loan, which is how we were able to get approved.

Both ratios are used to determine if you will qualify for a mortgage loan. Lenders will also use those ratios for other non-mortgage applications such as credit card, general loans, or any credit application you are seeking. The specific ratio numbers, as I will explain, relate strictly to mortgage loan applications. Let's start with GDS.

Your GDS lets a lender know what percentage of your gross income is used to service your housing expenses. You can calculate your gross debt service by first adding up your total housing expenses, which are mortgage payment, heating cost of the home, strata fee (50% only, don't ask why), and property tax. Then you take that number and divide it by your gross monthly income. The formula for calculating your gross debt service ratio is:

$$\frac{\text{Mortgage Payment + Heating + Strata (if applicable, only 50\%) + Property taxes}}{\text{Total Gross Monthly Income}[42]}$$

Here's an example to better understand the calculation. Ballian works for Canada Post as a Postal Delivery Officer. He's been with the company for five years and has an annual salary of $60,000. After five years of saving toward purchasing a home, he's finally found one he likes. The property he plans on buying will have a monthly mortgage payment of

---

42   "Debt Service Ratios – GDS and TDS," Ratehub, updated July 2, 2020, https://www.ratehub.ca/debt-service-ratios.

$2,500 (principal and interest), property tax of $250, strata fee of $350, and expected heating cost of $95, for a total monthly housing expense of $3,195. Based on that information, Ballian's gross debt service will be 60.40%. But what does that mean?

A GDS of 60.40% means he is allocating 60% of his gross monthly income toward his housing-related expenses. Said differently, Ballian spends 60% of his pre-tax income putting a roof over his head. Is that good or bad? From a mortgage loan application perspective, it's extremely high and will result in his application being declined. If someone is committing 60% of their gross income toward housing expenses, it doesn't give them much to live on. As such, mortgage loan applications have set ratios that applicants must meet to avoid such a situation. But before I provide you the number that lenders need you to meet, let's review the second ratio, TDS.

TDS allows a lender to determine how much of your gross income goes toward servicing your housing expenses and other debt obligations you have. Gross debt service only looks at the housing-related expenses. The formula for calculating your total debt service ratio is:

Mortgage Payment + Heating + Strata (if applicable, only 50%) + Property taxes + All Other Debt Expense/Obligations

Total Gross Monthly Income[43]

Let's continue with Ballian's example. In addition to the expenses already provided in the gross debt service section, Ballian has a car loan for $200 per month and credit card payment of $100 per month. He has no other debts besides those two items. Based on those two additional debts, his total monthly expense is now $3,495, which includes a monthly housing cost of $3,195. His monthly income is still $5,000 per month for total

---

43 Ibid.

debt service ratio of 66.40%, meaning Ballian spends 66% of his gross income to service his housing and other debts. Is this ratio good or bad? Again, from a mortgage application perspective, it's bad and will result in his application being declined by a lender.

Now that you know what GDS and TDS are, let's talk about the specific ratio numbers that lenders look for and for which you will have to be within to qualify for a mortgage loan.

Individuals seeking to obtain a mortgage loan must meet specific gross debt service and total debt service ratios set by lenders and mortgage insurers. In general, your gross debt service ratio should ideally be below 32% and no more than 39%, while your total debt service should ideally be below 42% and no more than 44%.[44]

LENDERS GDS/TDS RATIO REQUIREMENTS

GDS RATIO	TDS RATIO
High-Ratio Mortgage	High-Ratio Mortgage
32% but can go up to 39%	42% but can go up to 44%
Conventional Mortgage	Conventional Mortgage
32% but can go up to 39%	42% but can go up to 44%

44   Ibid.

Hitting these ratios doesn't mean you get an automatic approval from a lender. It just means you've likely met their respective GDS/TDS ratio requirement. Lenders are looking at your application based on all 5 C's, not just ratios, but you must hit their specific ratios to qualify. Lenders and insurers will sometimes make an exception to these ratios, but it's rare.

One other thing to know about these ratios is that private lenders who do not fall under government regulations set their own ratios, along with their own lending policy and guideline. A private lender is more concerned about security, as typically people use private lenders when their credit isn't great. Therefore, private lenders tend to want strong security (the home) along with a large down payment to reduce their risk exposure. It's best to try and get approval from an established lender as you will save money on the interest rate, and it's likely they will not overextend you as they have to follow certain regulations.

CHAPTER 13

MORTGAGE PRACTICE CASE STUDIES

t's finally time to put all the new knowledge you've learned to practice. This chapter is meant to enable you to practice through real cases that I worked on as an underwriter. Some of the information might seem crazy, but I assure you they are real. Of course, I have eliminated the borrower's name while also making some changes to the specific details around their application. After you've practiced with the cases, I will give you the actual end result of the case.

YOUNG BUYER

Tokyo is a 21-year-old man who managed to land a job working for his local municipal government. His position with the city is a temporary full-time maintenance staff, and he earns $29.16 per hour with a 40-hour work week. The last 24-month average income for him has been $50,461. Before landing the job with the city, Tokyo worked for a local well-known restaurant for a year as a server.

Tokyo has been living with his parents, and he is looking to get his own place. Tokyo has $14,000 saved up in his Registered Retirement Saving Plan (RRSP) and one large debt for $10,000 on his line of credit. Tokyo plans to use the $14,000 from his RRSP to pay off the line of credit and use the remaining cash for closing costs. His parents have agreed to gift him $35,000 toward his home purchase. His realtor has found a condo he likes at a purchase price of $266,000. Tokyo has secured a five-year mortgage term at 3% with a 25-year amortization. The lender's and insurer's maximum GDS is 39% and its maximum TDS is 44%. Below are additional details regarding his application.

Property Expense Details:

- Property tax of $727 per year
- Strata payment of $271 per month
- Heating cost of $75 per month
- Mortgage payment $1,127.09 per month (includes insurance premium)

Credit Profile:

- 650 credit score
- Credit card with balance of $311
- Line of credit with balance of $10,000
- Rent for $500 per month to parents

Formula Calculation

GDS

$$\frac{\text{Mortgage Payment + Heating + Strata (if applicable, only 50\%) + Property taxes}}{\text{Total Gross Monthly Income}^{45}}$$

TDS

$$\frac{\text{Mortgage Payment + Heating + Strata (if applicable, only 50\%) + Property taxes + All Other Debt Expense/Obligations}}{\text{Total Gross Monthly Income}}$$

Questions:

1. What is Tokyo's GDS and TDS ratios?

2. Does Tokyo's application meet the lender's requirements?

WHAT ACTUALLY HAPPENED

His application was declined by the insurer. During the application process, I discovered that Tokyo was actually a casual employee who recently became FT. While he had been employed there 24 months, he was only temporary FT the last six months before his mortgage application. The insurer did not feel comfortable using his two-year average as his letter of employment from his employer did not confirm minimum hours he was guaranteed, but rather he could work up to 40 hours per week. The other problem with the application was that his

---

45 "Debt Service Ratios – GDS and TDS," Ratehub, updated July 2, 2020, https://www.ratehub.ca/debt-service-ratios.

position was term-based, which meant after his current term was up in a few months, his employer was not obligated to rehire him.

The individual helping Tokyo with his mortgage application asked me to forward his application to another insurer for review. When sending a declined application to another insurer, the lender is required to disclose the reason for decline from the other insurer. The application was forwarded to another insurer, and it was also declined. The lender I worked for was not prepared to move forward with the application unless the loan could be insured. However, if an insurer was willing to take on the deal, I would have proceeded with the application.

CASE SOLUTION

Based on the information provided about Tokyo's application, his GDS is 33.25% and TDS is 33.47%, which would meet the lender's and insurer's guideline. I've tried to trick you on this application by giving you some of the information in yearly amount and others in monthly. You need to convert them to monthly to make things easier. I've also thrown in some other information to throw you off, such as Tokyo's rent payment to his parents. You would not include the rent payment as he's planning to purchase his own home, and therefore, he wouldn't have a rent payment upon moving. Tokyo was actually staying rent free with his parents according to his submission. You would also not include a payment for the line of credit debt as he will be paying that debt off before the mortgage funds.

My final take on this application was that the insurer did the right thing. Tokyo was just not ready yet to purchase a home as his job security wasn't as his application presented it upon further investigation. If the insurer did not decline the application, he might have bought a home that he wasn't ready for yet.

FIND THE SOLUTIONS ON THE NEXT PAGE! $\rightarrow$

GDS

$$\frac{\$1{,}127.09 + \$75 + \$135.50 + \$60.59}{\$4{,}205.08}$$

$$= \mathbf{33.25\%}$$

TDS

$$\frac{\$1{,}127.09 + \$75 + \$135.50 + \$60.59 + \$9.33}{\$4{,}205.08}$$

$$= \mathbf{33.47\%}$$

LOVE IS IN THE AIR

Lisbon and Porto are newlyweds who got married six months ago. It's Lisbon's second marriage after her divorce a few years ago. Porto works at a local brewery earning $45,058 annually. Lisbon works at a medical office as a permanent part-time receptionist earning $20,800 annually. Lisbon is currently on a maternity/parental leave and has been confirmed to return to work four months after the mortgage funds at the same annual salary of $20,800. The lender has accepted using Lisbon's full income as she will be returning to work. Their application also shows they receive a child tax credit for $1,880 per month. The lender allows the full child tax credit to be used for financing as long as supporting documents are provided to confirm payments. For their application, Lisbon has all the necessary documents required by the lender for her child tax credit income to be used for their application.

They are currently renting and would like to purchase a home for their expanding family. They currently have $10,000 saved and plan to borrow $15,000 from their line of credit to use toward the down payment, for a total of $25,000. They have found a home they like with a purchase price of $471,000. They are applying for a five-year, fixed-rate mortgage at 3% with a 25-year amortization. The lender and insurer GDS/TDS are 39/44 with minimum credit score of 630. Here are the additional application details.

Property Expense Details:

- ⊙ Property tax of $2,300 per year
- ⊙ Heating cost of $125 per month
- ⊙ Mortgage payment of $2,195.10 per month (includes insurance premium)
- ⊙ Credit Profile:
- ⊙ Lisbon: credit score of 696

- $\rightarrow$ Porto: credit score of 750
- $\rightarrow$ Credit card payment of $180 per month
- $\rightarrow$ Student loan of $241 per month
- $\rightarrow$ Line of credit payment of $450 per month ($15,000 being used for down payment)

Questions:

1. What is Lisbon and Porto's combined GDS and TDS for their application?

2. Is their application for an insured or uninsured mortgage application?

3. Will Lisbon and Porto meet the lender's/insurer's ratio guidelines?

WHAT ACTUALLY HAPPENED

Their application was approved. Lisbon and Porto's ratios were in line, and the insurer approved the application with their borrowed down payment. This file highlights how it's possible to be approved for something even when perhaps the more financially right thing to do is decline an application, regardless of whether the ratios are in line. In my opinion, they did not seem to be in a stable financial position yet, and I had concerns about their ability to meet their mortgage obligations. I also didn't like the fact they didn't have their down payment saved up. It seemed like they were simply trying to get a home when they were not financially there yet. However, if the ratios fit, it's much harder to decline a file as you enter a gray area. It's up to the applicant to really do their own due diligence on budget.

MORTGAGE PRACTICE CASE STUDIES

CASE SOLUTION

Lisbon and Porto's GDS is 34.09%; their TDS is 45.91%. Their application would be an insured mortgage as they are putting a down payment that's less than 20% of the purchase price. Based on the information I provide in the example, they would not qualify for their home purchase as their TDS ratio is outside the lender's and insurer's guidelines.

FIND THE SOLUTIONS ON THE NEXT PAGE! →

GDS

$$\frac{\$2{,}195.10 + \$125 + \$191.67}{\$7{,}368.16} = 34.09\%$$

TDS

$$\frac{\$2{,}195.10 + \$125 + \$191.67 + \$180 + \$241 + \$450}{\$7{,}368.16} = 45.91\%$$

THE FAMILY PURCHASE

Tofino and Sechelt are a couple in their mid-30s. They live with Tofino's parents in their basement suite. Recently, Sechelt's parents have had some health issues, and given that they are getting older, Sechelt would like to be closer to them to spend more time with them. They have decided to move to be closer to Sechelt's parents. Sechelt's parents are excited to have her closer to them, and they have agreed to assist them with their move by letting them live with them.

After making the move, Tofino has managed to find a job as chef with a local restaurant that will pay him $47,000 annually. Sechelt has decided to stay home with their three kids, but she gets $1,010 per month in child tax credit. After six months, they have decided to start looking for their own place. Sechelt's parents have agreed to help them make the purchase by gifting them $100,000 toward the down payment.

Their realtor has found a detached home they like that's close to Sechelt's parents. The home is listed at $484,000, and the realtor mentioned there is a suite they could rent out for $800. Sechelt and Tofino have applied for a five-year fixed-rate mortgage at 3.8% with an amortization of 25 years. The lender allows rental income to be used at 50% of the expected rental income, which is added as additional income. The lender allows the full child tax credit income to be used as long as kids are under 12 years of age, and all three kids are under 8 years of age. Both the lender's and insurer's maximum GDS/TDS are 39/44. The lender's and insurer's minimum credit score is 600. Here are additional details about their application.

Property Expense Details:

- → Property tax of $2,000 per year
- → Heating of $1,200 per year
- → Mortgage payment of $1,978.50 per month

Credit Profile:

- ⊕ Both have limited to no credit history
- ⊕ Credit score for both is 600
- ⊕ Tofino has a cellphone account reporting on credit bureau only
- ⊕ Sechelt has one credit card with zero balance

Questions:

1. What is Tofino and Sechelt's GDS and TDS?
2. Will Tofino and Sechelt's mortgage application be approved?

WHAT ACTUALLY HAPPENED

This application was eventually approved, but some changes were required to the initial submission. When the appraisal for the property was completed along with economic rents (i.e., how much the suite could rent for), some discrepancies were discovered.

The listing advised there was a basement suite, but upon inspection it turned out it wasn't really a basement suite as it didn't even have a proper kitchen. The kitchen contained only a small portable kitchen burner. At the time of the application, most suites were legal non-confirming, which means they were built for the most part like a legal suite but didn't get a permit from their local municipality, as it was costly and timely. Lenders would accept the rents as long as it was a self-contained suite from the main house. This particular home didn't meet such guidelines. The other issue with this application was their credit profile, along with the fact their entire down payment was gifted. The application was initially declined due to weak overall credit and not having an actual suite, which brought the ratios outside the guidelines.

They required additional down payment to make the deal work. Sechelt's parents decided to add their name to the application as borrowers rather

MORTGAGE PRACTICE CASE STUDIES

than give them additional down payment. The application was then approved as her parents had a strong pension and good self-employed business income. The only other issue was the parents didn't want to go on the title, which was eventually agreed to, but would be guarantors of the loan. They were okay with that stipulation because they no longer had to put down the large $100,000 down payment since the combined income of all parties allowed for a much lower down payment.

CASE SOLUTION

You should have Sechelt and Tofino's GDS as 45.57% with their TDS being the same since they had no other debts. Based on the lender's and insurer's guideline provided in the example, their application would not have been approved as their GDS and TDS ratios doesn't fit the respective guidelines provided in the example.

FIND THE SOLUTIONS ON THE NEXT PAGE! →

GDS

$$\frac{\$1,978.50 + \$100 + \$166.67}{\$4,926.66}$$

$$= 45.57\%$$

TDS

$$\frac{\$1,978.50 + \$100 + \$166.67}{\$4,926.66}$$

$$= 45.57\%$$

Mortgage poverty is not being able to do anything other than paying your mortgage payments.

The next seven chapters are things you should know to help you avoid mortgage poverty.

CHAPTER 14

STEP ONE IN AVOIDING MORTGAGE POVERTY

I n my first real estate transaction, I didn't fully understand the fundamental drivers of real estate prices. To be honest, I didn't really care. I just wanted a nice home and didn't want to be house poor. Some of my clients at the bank were real estate investors, and they often would speak in general terms about real estate investing. However, I wasn't really a real estate advisor and was more interested in stocks. But upon becoming a homeowner, I became very much interested in what drove real estate prices up or down since I had a selfish interest in it going up. I wish I paid more attention to what drove real estate values as I think, from a financial position, I could have made a better purchase in terms of investment with our initial home.

Understanding real estate drivers is important as they enable you to see when the real estate system is operating as it should and when it's not operating according to the fundamentals. That's why you have to at least familiarize yourself with the fundamental drivers if you're purchasing real estate especially when the price point is much higher, which means the mortgage debt required to finance home purchases is greater. To understand if a system isn't operating well, you first need to understand how the system should work in the first place. As such, I will try and give you a basic understanding of the fundamentals that should drive the real estate market. The explanation should enable you to determine if the prices you are seeing or willing to pay are supported by the fundamentals or if it's simply emotional irrationality.

SUPPLY AND DEMAND

This real estate driver is one of the most well-known and understood. If there are a lot of homes for sale and few buyers who want those homes, then the prices for those homes will have to come down to attract the buyers. When there is an excess supply of a product, prices normally come down until an equilibrium price level is achieved again.

The opposite can happen on the buyer side as well. If there are a lot of homebuyers and few homes available for sale, home prices generally will rise. As a result of the low supply of homes, prospective homebuyers are more likely to pay more for the home in an effort to secure the home they desire. When multiplied over and over, the effect eventually drives home prices up until a new equilibrium price is set.[46]

EMPLOYMENT CONDITIONS

Employment conditions speak to the general strength of the economy. The biggest indicator often sighted for the health of the economy is the employment rate. A high unemployment rate usually means the economy

---

46   "How Does Supply and Demand Affect the Housing Market?" Investopedia, updated September 2, 2020, https://www.investopedia.com/ask/answers/040215/how-does-law-supply-and-demand-affect-housing-market.asp.

isn't doing well, while a low unemployment rate is generally associated with a strong economy.[47]

Investors are more likely to build homes when the economy is doing well. The cycle makes sense because if the economy isn't doing well, the investor will have a lower demand for their homes upon completion. If the employment is high, potential buyers are more likely to want to buy a home or spend more in general.

INTEREST RATES

Interest rates speak to liquidity of credit along with affordability. On July 31, 1981, Canada's prime mortgage rate was 21.75%, which is drastically higher than the mortgage prime rate of 2.45% as of August 31, 2021.[48] If the current interest rate is high, as it was in 1981, then the mortgage payments for homeowners will also be high. If people can't afford or qualify for the mortgage payments because of high mortgage interest rates, then home prices generally should come down because people need a lower price point to counteract high mortgage rates. On the other side, if interest rates are low, then people can qualify for higher mortgage payments due to low-interest mortgage rates. Therefore, they can pay a higher price for a home, which results in higher home prices. The cycle used to vary up and down, but we've been in a low interest rate environment pretty much since the Great Recession in 2008,[49] and I'm not sure if the economy as a whole can really handle high interest rates ever again, as the impact of high interest rates would be extremely detrimental to the Canadian economy and to the world.

---

47   Elvis Picardo, "How the Unemployment Rate Affects Everybody," Investopedia, updated September 24, 2020, https://www.investopedia.com/articles/economics/10/unemployment-rate-get-real.asp.

48   "Prime Mortgage Rate History," Ratehub, accessed August 13, 2021, https://www.ratehub.ca/prime-mortgage-rate-history.

49   John Weinberg, "The Great Recession and its Aftermath," Federal Reserve History, November 22, 2013, https://www.federalreservehistory.org/essays/great-recession-and-its-aftermath.

I tend to pay close attention to interest rates and people's general confidence about the economy to get a clear sense of where the real estate market is heading. While the previous economic indicators I mentioned are important, ease of credit is what I really pay attention to. Ease of credit for me simply means how easily people are able to qualify for a mortgage and how easy it is for people to access credit. For example, if the mortgage rules and guideline around qualification are made easier, then the ability of people to obtain a mortgage loan will be easier. Therefore, they will be able to bid up prices more as they can qualify more easily. The opposite can happen when mortgage rules are tightened and people are not able to qualify as easily, which likely will result in lower or flat house prices.

Why is that factor important? In the real world, people without jobs will borrow money regardless of whether they can afford the debt as long as someone is willing to provide them credit. Individuals who have a job are likely to borrow more if the process to obtain credit is easy, which can result in their overextending themselves due to the easy access to credit.

You should learn to put actual human behavior on top of economic expectations to really understand real world economics.

GOVERNMENT POLICIES

Governments also play a role in home prices. In general, the roles tend to be positive toward homeownership. As of 2016, 63% of Canadian families owned their own principal residence.[50] Given the large percentage of Canadian families who own their home, it's good politics to craft policy that encourages and supports homeownership in general regardless of the political stripe shown by opposing political parties. During the 2015 Canadian federal election, the Conservative government campaigned

---

50 Sharanjit Uppal, "Homeownership, mortgage debt and types of mortgage among Canadian families," Statistics Canada, August 8, 2019, https://www150.statcan.gc.ca/n1/pub/75-006-x/2019001/article/00012-eng.htm.

to increase the amount first-time homebuyers could withdraw from their RRSP from $25,000 to $35,000.[51] Most recently in 2019, the Liberal government introduced a shared equity mortgage program to be administered through Canada Mortgage and Housing Corporation (CMHC) to assist first-time homebuyers in purchasing their first home.[52] Government policies tend to support homeownership as homeowners tend to have a higher voting rate than renters, which was shown in the 2011 Canadian election. It makes good political sense to keep that voting block happy.[53]

But government can also have a negative impact on prices and purchasers. In Canada in 2018, the Office of the Superintendent of Financial Institutions (OSFI) introduced a stress test referred to as B20, which required potential homebuyers to be able to qualify for the home they wish to purchase at a higher interest rate. The policy was intended to create financial stability by ensuring borrowers were not overextending themselves and was recently updated on June 1, 2021. Superintendent Jeremy Rudin is quoted as saying, "Sound residential mortgage underwriting is always important for the safety and stability of financial institutions; today it is more important than ever."[54]

Governments can also impact home prices through tax policies, both positively and/or negatively. Recently the provincial government of

51 "Stephen Harper pledges higher RRSP withdrawal limit for 1st time homebuyers," CBC News, updated August 12, 2015, https://www.cbc.ca/news/politics/stephen-harper-pledges-higher-rrsp-withdrawal-limit-for-1st-time-homebuyers-1.3188580.

52 "First-Time Home Buyer Incentive," Government of Canada National Housing Strategy, accessed August 13, 2021, https://www.placetocallhome.ca/fthbi/first-time-homebuyer-incentive.

53 Sharanjit Uppal and Sébastien LaRochelle-Côté, "Factors associated with voting," *Perspectives on Labour and Income*, February 24, 2012, https://www150.statcan.gc.ca/n1/pub/75-001-x/2012001/article/11629-eng.pdf.

54 "OSFI proposes new minimum qualifying rate for uninsured mortgages," Office of the Superintendent of Financial Institutions, April 8, 2021, https://www.osfi-bsif.gc.ca/Eng/osfi-bsif/med/Pages/b20-nr.aspx.

Ontario and British Columbia passed a foreign buyer's tax in an effort to cool foreign ownership in their respective residential market.[55]

IMMIGRATION AND TRANSPORTATION

From a housing perspective, immigration is important for both supply and demand, especially in Canada. New people moving to Canada creates an increase in the demand for housing.

In the short run, the demand puts pressure on prices as it outweighs the supply. Housing supply will have to be increased to meet the demand to bring the market back to an equilibrium. CHMC published a report titled "Migration Trends in Most Populated CMAs (2002 – 2019)," which found that Canada's home prices surged in Canada's biggest housing market of Vancouver and Toronto in 2015 and 2019, with high immigration playing a role in that price increase.[56] The impact makes sense when you think about it. If current housing supply isn't meeting local demand but the government brings in more people (demand), then you create an environment where many people need homes, but not enough homes are available. Therefore, prices increase as people bid up prices in an effort to secure the home they desire.

However, the solution to an increased housing demand problem isn't to cut off immigration. Indeed, the government's intention for migration isn't to help the housing market, but rather the Canadian economy as a whole. A constant flow of immigration to Canada is particularly important given Canada's low population, which as of April 1, 2021,

55 "B.C. areas for the additional property transfer tax," British Columbia, accessed August 13, 2021, https://www2.gov.bc.ca/gov/content/taxes/property-taxes/property-transfer-tax/additional-property-transfer-tax/bc-areas.

56 "Migration Trends in Most Popular CMAs (2002 – 2019)," CMHC, March 4, 2021, https://www.cmhc-schl.gc.ca/en/blog/2021/migration-trends-most-populated-cmas-2002-2019.

was estimated at 38,131,104.[57] Canada also has a low total fertility rate (TFR), which was at 1.47 births per woman in 2019 compared to 3.94 in 1959.[58] According to Statistics Canada, "Canada's TFR has been below the replacement rate of 2.1 births per women since 1971, meaning that the number of babies being born is not enough for the current population to replace itself."[59] Therefore, immigration isn't really an option but a requirement for the economy to function, which unintentionally also keeps house prices increasing as supply of homes isn't meeting the demand created by this immigration need.

On to the transportation side's effect on home prices. Increased rapid transportation generally results in people being able to live farther away from their work or the main city. With home prices typically less in suburban areas, the availability of transportation options generally helps both the supply and demand side of housing.

---

57   "Canada's population estimates, first quarter 2021," Statistics Canada, June 17, 2021, https://www150.statcan.gc.ca/n1/daily-quotidien/210617/dq210617c-eng.htm?lnk=dai-quo&indid=4098-1&indgeo=0.

58   "Births, 2019," Statistics Canada, September 29, 2020, https://www150.statcan.gc.ca/n1/daily-quotidien/200929/dq200929e-eng.htm.

59   Ibid.

CHAPTER 15

WHY YOU SHOULDN'T GET A MORTGAGE PRE-APPROVAL

When I worked at the bank, I was trained to use pre-approval as a conversation document with clients about homeownership. However, most of the people I assisted already had their mind made up about buying a home and came to me to simply confirm their loan amount. They weren't really interested in talking about homeownership. Moreover, I often found the document resulted in most of my clients going out to shop for a home even when we agreed that doing the pre-approval was simply to be used as a means to discuss their home purchase in more detail. That's largely the problem with pre-approvals: They can be a great tool, but you have to be disciplined in using it the right way.

A pre-approval is a document that a lender provides based on the information they are provided by the borrower, which estimates the total mortgage they can afford.[60] The document is usually based on a specific rate that is guaranteed anywhere from 90 days to 120 days depending on the lender.

Pre-approval isn't the same thing as being approved for a mortgage loan.[61] A mortgage application requires an actual credit application, identifiable security, and typically approvals are for 90 days only, with some exceptions. Lenders do not want to give you an approval for longer than 90 days because a lot can change in 90 days. Even if a lender provides an approval longer than 90 days, they typically will add a condition advising that they can revisit your application closer to funding to ensure there hasn't been any major material changes to your application.

Since a credit application is not actually undertaken during most pre-approvals, most lenders do not do a credit check as it would be a pointless hit on someone's credit, especially when they might not buy for several months or years. Instead, the lender simply takes some information from the potential borrower such as income level, debt obligation, desired purchase price of home, along with current interest rate, and provides the borrower with an idea of the maximum dollar amount they can afford along with the interest rate that is guaranteed for a specific period.

The pre-approval mortgage application has been marketed as a "must have" document if you are truly serious about buying a home. I agree, but I object to its usage within the industry. It's a conversation document, the intent of which has been lost on all parties involved in the homeownership process.

The idea behind a mortgage pre-approval is to have a conversation about your finances and less about knowing what you can qualify for. The

---

60 https://www.canada.ca/en/financial-consumer-agency/services/mortgages/preapproval-qualify-mortgage.html

61 Ibid.

document is meant to force you to sit down with someone and really go over your finances and see if you are ready to buy a home, not to discuss your rate or how much of a home you can buy.

Today, however, most people never talk about their finances. Instead, most call up their lender or broker and advise them they would like to be pre-approved. The lender or broker simply takes some input data, and some might actually do a credit check to make the pre-approval feel more real. The borrower is then offered a document that says they have been approved for a certain mortgage amount and implies that they should go find their dream home.

No other conversation is discussed for the most part. No discussion about what your plans are for the next five years. Do you see yourself in the same job? What is the amount of emergency savings you have? Do you have enough to cover ongoing operating costs of a home? Interestingly, 50% of homebuyers in the 2018 Mortgage Consumer Survey confirmed that their mortgage professional didn't discuss unexpected home costs with them.[62] Those aspects are not discussed with most pre-approvals. Instead, all everyone wants to know is how much can they afford and what interest rate can they secure.

Mortgage pre-approvals tend to function more as a psychological commitment document because it encourages you to commit to homeownership even if you might actually not be ready for it. Once the pre-approval document is offered to you it becomes a self-fulfilling prophesy, and you're off to the races.

You should use a pre-approval as a means to have a meaningful discussion about housing and what you want your life to look like from a financial

---

62 "2018 Mortgage Consumer Survey: Home Buyers," CMHC, October 15, 2018, https://eppdscrmssa01.blob.core.windows.net/cmhcprodcontainer/sf/project/cmhc/pdfs/content/en/mcs-homebuyers-2018.pdf?sv=2020-02-10&ss=b&srt=sco&sp=r&se=2024-03-30T20:07:16Z&st=2021-03-30T12:07:16Z&spr=https&sig=zphoCuN3v1pBl42RCAx1Eaitv CCwi6S7%2BcL5IgMH2RY%3D.

standpoint. You have to control the conversation and deal with someone who is equally ready to take the time to discuss the details about the true cost of homeownership. If you do that fact-finding, then the pre-approval works well, and it will be one of the best things you've done to increase your chances of being successful with your home purchase.

CHAPTER 16

YOUR HOME IS NOT AN INVESTMENT

I f a homeowner wants to be successful in their real estate purchase, then they first must accept the reality that they are not investors but rather an individual seeking shelter in the form of homeownership. As such, they must not heed the often talked about slogan regarding their home being an asset; rather, they must instead think of their home purchase as a lifestyle purchase. The associated mortgage attached to the homeowner's home will determine the type of lifestyle the applicant and their family will have.

When you look at a home, disregard its beauty and all the emotional traps set by other human beings who are looking to sell you the false front that they call assets. I want you to ask yourself this simple question: What type of lifestyle will the mortgage required to buy this home afford me and those I love? Is that a lifestyle I am prepared to live for the next 25 years?

If you approach your purchase that way, then you will have the mindset of a homeowner rather than one wanting to be a real estate investor. The homeowner's mindset is one smartly focused on providing a particular lifestyle desired for themselves and those they love. The home is simply a shelter to create lasting memories, not about real estate investing. That outcome will be far more valuable to them than making a good return.

Let's assume you've found the perfect house. You like the house, and it's in a great neighborhood. Your realtor advises you that it's a great buy, and it will go up in value overtime. Stop! Disregard that last comment by your realtor. The realtor is creating an investor mindset, but you are not seeking to be a real estate investor. The realtor has no clue they are doing that (I hope). You are not an investor, but rather a homeowner seeking a reasonable shelter for you and your family. Now, let's assume the mortgage payments are within your affordable budget. Should you purchase the home? The common practice is if you can afford it, you should buy it. But remember that the bank, as I've already shown you, only looks at one small part of your true expenses. They do not account for your entire lifestyle at time of application or in the future.

That's why you should ask yourself what kind of lifestyle will this mortgage afford me, and am I prepared to live that lifestyle for the next 25 years? Framing it that way forces you to really ask yourself if you will be able to do the things you want even with this mortgage. Will you be able to travel? Will you be able to spend time with those you love? Will you be able to start a family or continue to raise your family? Will you even be able to afford the mortgage payment if your job situation changes? Do you even like your job? Will you be able to continue to invest in yourself today and in the future? Does this home provide the space you need today and potential additional space in the future if things change? Will this mortgage allow you to save for retirement? Will you be able to save for your kids' education with this mortgage? Will this mortgage allow you and your spouse to pay for daycare if you decided to have kids? Will this mortgage allow you to pursue other career opportunities?

Those are just some of the questions you should be thinking about. If it seems like a lot, that's the point. When you think of the life you want, you won't fall for the idea that you need to buy a house at any cost because it becomes clear you cannot eat your home for food.

Take a deep breath because you and your family truly need to ask yourselves, what type of lifestyle do you want and does this mortgage enable you to do that today? Or, will it prevent you from doing that simply so that you can say you own a home?

CHAPTER 17

BANKS MAKE MONEY WHEN YOU REFINANCE

O ne of my many frustrations while working at the bank was the revolving refinance applications I often dealt with. There seemed to be a disconnect between what people wanted from a refinance versus what they actually accomplished. For the most part, clients came to me seeking cash flow relief along with interest saving. However, what they actually did was obtain cash flow relief at the expense of amortizing their debt over a longer period while increasing their overall mortgage debt—and in most cases increased interest costs. I tried to explain the impact to clients, but often I was unsuccessful until I realized the disconnect between what clients wanted versus what their refinancing application actually accomplished. Enter marketing ploys.

Lenders have done a terrific job when it comes to marketing of mortgage refinances, especially through the home equity line of credit (HELOC) product. They have been able to convince homeowners that taking equity from their home to pay off debt is always a good idea. Convenience has once again won against practicing good financial behavior.

A home equity line of credit is convenient, and given its convenience, people utilize it for pretty much anything. Its uses can range from investing to buying underwear. I'm not judging, just simply highlighting the range of use.

Lenders have further added to the convenience of completing a mortgage refinance or obtaining a home equity line of credit product by making either one easier, faster, and cheaper. In doing so, lenders have really stacked the deck against homeowners and made the refinancing temptation just too hard to pass up.

In the past when you purchased a home, you had to go to a lawyer or notary to register the mortgage loan charged on the title. This charge was set for the exact loan amount you owed the bank. For example, if it was a $300,000 loan, the mortgage charge on title would be registered for $300,000. If after three years into your five-year mortgage term, you decided to refinance the property to take advantage of increasing home prices to pull out some equity, you would have to make another trip to the lawyer or notary to register the new loan amount. As a result of having to re-register the charge, you would have to pay the lawyer or notary again to register the new charge. That cost often meant it wasn't really worth the effort to, say, pay $1,500 to the lawyer to only obtain an additional $15,000 in new equity. That fact gave people reason to think twice about their refinance before proceeding. Most people likely would do a cost-benefit analysis before proceeding with the refinance.

Today, however, almost all lenders have what's known as a collateral charge mortgage. A collateral mortgage allows a lender to continue to refinance the mortgage without requiring a lawyer or notary to re-register the charge each time you refinance your property. It's a game changer that's more or less the standard way of registering all mortgage charges today.

All that convenience coupled with the ease to access equity from your home means most homeowners will easily take all the gains from their property and give them back to the lender, who then charges them more interest for the privilege of accessing those funds.

In CMHC's Mortgage Consumer Survey for both 2018 and 2019, the most common reason for refinance was debt consolidation.[63] The survey found 26% of homeowners surveyed in 2019 confirmed they were obtaining HELOC (which is a form of refinance) based on the recommendation of their bank, lawyer, or broker.[64] Many homeowners don't understand that they are taking out their gains from their home and simply giving it back to the lender. That net loss is why you have to stop refinancing your home frequently. In fact, you really should entirely avoid refinancing your property.

When you purchase your home, you do so by borrowing money from a lender. The lender charges you interest on the principal amount it lends you to be able to purchase the home. You agree to the terms of the mortgage lender and make interest and principal payments to get the loan you need to purchase the home.

Lenders love the deal because they get a steady stream of revenue from your principal and interest payments. The principal goes toward the original loan they lent you (covering their capital) while the interest is income to them on the loan.

---

63 "2018 Mortgage Consumer Survey: Refinancers," CMHC, October 15, 2018, https://eppdscrmssa01.blob.core.windows.net/cmhcprodcontainer/sf/project/cmhc/pdfs/content/en/mcs-refinancers-2018.pdf?sv=2020-02-10&ss=b&srt=sco&sp=r&se=2024-03-30T20:07:16Z&st=2021-03-30T12:07:16Z&spr=https&sig=zphoCuN3v1pBl42RCAx1EaitvCCwi6S7%2BcL5IgMH2RY%3D; "The State of Homebuying in Canada: 2019 CMHC Mortgage Consumer Survey."

64 "The State of Homebuying in Canada: 2019 CMHC Mortgage Consumer Survey."

You, as the homeowner, agree to their terms because eventually you will pay off the original loan along with the interest payment owed. But in addition to paying it off, you also have the possibility of seeing your property appreciate over time. When the property appreciates, your investment turns more positive, especially if it exceeds the total cost of your home, including interest owed. Therefore, when you refinance your property, you are adding to the original purchase cost of your home.

A refinance is essentially you taking away from whatever profit you've made on your home, then giving that back to the lender, and, worse, letting them charge you more interest to utilize those funds! Since the number one reason people refinance is for debt consolidation, they take the gain from their property and use it to pay off more debt, which increases their overall home investment cost while reducing their overall rate of return. Those effects are why refinancing a principal residence for non-income adding purposes is a bad thing.

What's even worse is that most people repeat the process the minute they have a slight increase in the equity of their home. In the CMHC 2019 Mortgage Consumer Survey, 52% of the respondents said it was their first time completing a refinance.[65] Since we know that debt consolidation is the number one reason why homeowners refinance, it's fair to say the vast majority of those refinances that year were likely for debt consolidation. Yet, those homeowners actually increased their debt!

It's almost a sleight of hand because when it comes to debt consolidation refinance, lenders make homeowners feel as though they are doing a good thing by moving their high credit card debt to a lower interest rate product such as the mortgage or home equity line of credit. What they fail to point out to the homeowner is that they are taking all the gains you've made on the home, increasing your interest cost, and all the

---

65 Ibid.

while making the lender wealthier, as now they will receive a higher total interest payment from you. The best part for the lender is when they put the new funds in a product that gives you the option to pay interest only, such as an equity line of credit, which ensures you will never pay down the principal but will also give them a steady stream of income.

HARDLY ANY GOOD REASONS TO REFINANCE

One worthwhile purpose to a refinance is if you don't take the equity in your home but are getting a lower rate at the same or fewer mortgage term years. Even with those conditions, however, the expenses of refinancing need to be considered as they might seriously impact the benefit.

The other worthwhile purpose to a refinance is if you are using it to produce an income stream. Investors refinance their property to invest in the market, buy a business, or buy another investment property with an income stream, while homeowners refinance for debt consolidation. Investors understand that if they take out a loan on a home, they should use the proceeds to invest in something that can generate a higher return now and in the long run. If they cannot find such an investment, then they simply leave the equity in the home.

Lenders do a terrible job, however, of helping homeowners understand the difference between their situation and those of investors. In fact, lenders give homeowners the illusion they are tackling their debt when they often are doing the opposite.

Let's use an example to illustrate what I mean. Assume you have a mortgage for $300,000 with a five-year term at 3% with a 25-year amortization. Let's disregard all other expenses associated with the home and assume the only other debt you have is a car loan for $25,000 with a monthly payment of $340.84 based on an annual interest rate of 7% with an eight-year loan term. After two years into your car loan, you're feeling cash flow poor. Your car loan is a huge monthly payment, and you think paying it off sooner would give you a lot of free cash flow. You believe that if you could move the car loan debt into your mortgage you would save on interest cost as you would only be paying 3% at current market rate rather than the 7% interest rate of your existing car loan. The total amount to be paid back on your car loan is $32,721 (interest and principal) for the full eight years. At the start of year three, your current balance owed on the car loan is $19,992. Let's visualize the current situation I'm describing before we move forward.

PRODUCT	TERM	RATE	AMORTIZATION/ TERM
Mortgage	5 years	3%	25 years
Car Loan	8 years	7%	8 years

MONTHLY PAYMENT	BALANCE OF AFTER 24 MONTHS	BALANCE OWED AT THE END OF MORTGAGE/LOAN TERM
$1,419.74	$283,343*	$256,423*
$340.84	$19,992*	$32,721*

*Balances have not been rounded and do not include cents.

So, you approach your lender and go over your situation. The lender or professional you are working with agrees with your uninformed assessment of your financial situation and claims that a refinance would be the smart thing to do. They confirm to you that you would be saving interest cost as you would move your car loan that's currently at 7% and add it to your mortgage loan, which is at a lower interest rate of 3%, saving both interest cost and improving your cash flow at the same time. On the surface, the rationalization appears to be true. You are saving interest cost and also getting cash flow relief. But on further investigation you can see with the chart below that you actually end up costing yourself more money in the long run. The reason for that outcome is what I stated earlier at the start of this chapter: When it comes to refinance, people are often unclear as to what they actually want to accomplish with their refinance and what they are actually doing with their refinance. Below is what the newly refinanced mortgage will look like after it's completed while rounding the total refinance loan amount to $303,335 ($283,343 + $19,992).

PRODUCT	TERM	RATE	AMORTIZATION
Newly Refinanced Mortgage	5 years	3%	25 years

MONTHLY PAYMENT	TOTAL TERM AMOUNT OWED	CASH FLOW RELIEF
$1,435.52	$259,274*	$325.06

* Balances have not been rounded and do not include cents.

After refinancing the car loan into the mortgage loan, the total mortgage amount is now $303,335. Since the mortgage has been refinanced for a new five-year term and payments have been re-amortized back to 25 years, the actual mortgage payment increased slightly while the monthly cash flow relief works out to be $325.06, which is the difference between the original mortgage payment plus the car loan payment minus the new mortgage payment of $1,435.52.

But here's what you don't see or what the lower interest rate and lower monthly combined payment doesn't show with your car loan refinanced into your mortgage:

PRODUCT	AMORTIZATION/ TERM	RATE	LOAN AMOUNT
Original Car Loan	8 years	7%	$25,000
Car Loan Cost Refinanced into Mortgage	25 years	3%	$19,992

MONTHLY PAYMENT	TOTAL AMOUNT PAID	TOTAL INTEREST PAID
$340.84	$32,721*	$7,721*
$94.61	$28,383*	$8,391*

*Balances have not been rounded and do not include cents.

In our example, the client wasn't looking to pay more for his car loan, at least that wasn't his intention. However, that's what he ends up doing with his refinance. Furthermore, he's increased the actual years it will take for him to pay off his mortgage by re-amortizing his mortgage back to 25 years. Remember, he commenced his refinance at the start of his third year, which means he should have kept his amortization at 23 years. By resetting his amortization, he actually has a real amortization of 27 years.

The monthly combined amount of $1,435 looked good as it hides the car loan refinance details within the mortgage payment. The reason most people get into this situation is that they do not know that by rolling the car loan into their mortgage they lock in the term of their car loan from 8 years to 25 years, which isn't their intention. However, to sell the refinance, the lender will focus on the comparison on paper to show cash flow relief along with the lower interest rate. To maximize the lender's cash flow relief argument, they maximized the amortization possible to give you the lowest possible payment, which provides the cash flow, but in this example, results in your paying for that cash flow with a higher overall interest payment over the 25-year period.

To avoid losing money, you simply should keep paying the same monthly amount of your car's original loan, which means the mortgage payment actually goes up, and then after the eight-year mark, by which your car loan was set to be paid off, you can drop the mortgage payment back down as you've now paid down the car loan debt portion while saving interest by paying only 3% versus the original 7%. While the immediate cash flow improvement isn't realized, in the long run you'll come out ahead.

That tactic to truly save by refinancing isn't communicated, unfortunately, to most borrowers, and therefore, most people who refinance do not fully understand the complete picture of what they have done. I doubt anyone wants to pay more interest on their car loan and would rather have the debt paid off sooner than extend it for 25 years for a small cash flow relief, which comes at the expense of increased interest amount overall. At least, they should be told the complete picture to make a more informed decision. What makes the situation worse is that the refinance proceeds were used to pay off a depreciating asset, which means you've taken on additional interest cost on an asset that will not go up in value.

It's a sad cycle that will continue until the lenders put homeowners' overall financial wealth first and tell them there are no shortcuts to paying off debt.

LEARN THE LESSON

Most homeowners already cannot afford the lifestyle their mortgage provides them as shown in the 2019 Mortgage Consumer Survey, which found 23% of homebuyers said their current level of debt is higher than they expected—an increase from 19% in 2018.[66] As a result, homeowners get in trouble by having to borrow to provide the things they might want or need that their mortgage debt prevents them from having.

The best method to avoid frequent refinance is to take the information you've learned in this book and ensure the mortgage you get doesn't prevent you from doing the things you enjoy. If you can't do what you enjoy due to your mortgage debt, you're likely to consider refinancing as a means to fund your lifestyle. With the exception noted previously, my advice is to avoid refinancing at all costs, as doing so will extend your mortgage obligation with little gain to you but to the delight of your lender.

---

66 "Survey Results 2018," CMHC, October 18, 2018, https://www.cmhc-schl.gc.ca/en/
professionals/housing-markets-data-and-research/housing-research/surveys/mortgage-
consumer-surveys/survey-results-2018.; Ibid.

CHAPTER 18

THE TRUE COST
OF YOUR HOME
(NOT WHAT THE BANK SAYS)

Besides controlling your emotions, one of the challenges with buying a home wisely is the overload of information that you have to sort through. As a first-time homeowner who worked at a bank, I felt overwhelmed with the amount of information that I had to find. That feeling of being overwhelmed is why I took the time before even seeing a home to ensure the numbers made sense. At the time, I simply input the numbers into an Excel spreadsheet to ensure that after we covered all the housing expenses, we were left with enough to live our normal lives while continuing to invest in the future.

Today, there is more information available about homeownership and mortgages than ever, which makes it even more difficult to focus. So, I want to provide a quick formula that you can start with to quickly see how much of your income is being used to provide a roof over your head while also capturing the complete cost of your home purchase. Please remember this formula is designed to be a starting point, not a start and end point when purchasing or refinancing your home.

When we got our first mortgage, I wasn't told what the final ratios were for our mortgage GDS or TDS. If you were to ask most homeowners what their GDS or TDS was when they got their mortgage, there's a high probability many do not know.

It's a sad truth as we all should know how much of our income is going toward putting a roof over our heads. However, another sad truth is most of us are only interested in being approved when it comes to our mortgages and care less about if we can truly afford the mortgage. I believe everyone needs a roof over their head, but I don't believe that a home with a mortgage is the only option to provide that roof.

Now that you know how to calculate GDS and TDS, let's utilize your knowledge about those ratios to help you calculate your true and total mortgage cost. While GDS/TDS ratios are a good starting point, you shouldn't base your budgeting or buying decisions solely on them. Lender ratios are only important for qualifying for a mortgage.

One of the main problems with GDS/TDS ratio is it's based on the homeowner's gross income before taxes, not the realistic take home pay of the borrower. If you're like me, you pay taxes, and your take home pay isn't the same as your gross income. That's why I want to introduce two new ratios that you should use, which I call Net Gross Debt Service ratio (NGDS) and Net Total Debt Service ratio (NTDS). I know, it's not as easy or as marketable as GDS/TDS but call it whatever you wish as long as you follow my steps in how to calculate the ratios.

The calculations are similar to GDS/TDS ratios formula with a couple of tweaks. First, you will use your net after-tax income rather than your gross income. Instead of plugging in your gross income in the denominator, plug the actual income you get in your bank account each month after all deductions have been taken. The second difference is to take into account your full housing expenses and 100% of any strata or homeowner association fees.

Just to repeat, here's what the GDS formula looks like for the lender:

$$\frac{\text{Mortgage Payment + Heating + Strata (if applicable, only 50\%) + Property Taxes}}{\text{Total Gross Monthly Income (before taxes and payroll expenses are deducted)}}$$

Here's my updated NGDS formula you should use:

$$\frac{\text{Mortgage Payment + Heating + Strata (if applicable, 100\%) + Property Taxes + City Water/Garbage + Home Insurance}}{\text{Total Net Monthly Income (after taxes and payroll expenses have been deducted)}}$$

I've added city water/garbage costs to your NGDS as they are costs you might have to pay as part of owing your home. You might have to estimate those costs or contact your local city to obtain their estimates. I recommend you add any other known expenses to the NTDS section. This updated formula should capture the true cost of your housing-related expenses and give you a quick and clearer picture of how much of your take home pay is actually going toward putting a roof over your head.

Next, let's update the TDS ratios used by lenders, which is currently the following formula:

$$\frac{\text{Mortgage Payment + Heating + Strata (if applicable, only 50\%) + Property Taxes + All Other Expenses (told to lender or found on credit report)}}{\text{Total Gross Monthly Income (before taxes and payroll expenses are deducted)}}$$

Here's my NTDS formula you should use for yourself:

$$\frac{\text{Mortgage Payment + Heating + Strata (if applicable, 100\%) + Property Taxes + City Water/Garbage + Home Insurance + All Expenses (found on your credit report) + All Real-Life Expenses (known to you and not known to the lender)}}{\text{Total Net Monthly Income (after taxes and payroll expenses have been deducted)}}$$

I've added one new category to calculating your NTDS, which is "real life" expenses. These are essentially all the expenses you need to pay to maintain the lifestyle you want today and in the future. Remember, for the most part, lenders will only take debts you let them know about, they discover, or they find on the credit report at the time of your application. They don't look into other expenses in terms of the true cost of your mortgage obligation on the quality of your life.

The NTDS ratio captures the entire picture and will show how much of your net income is or will be spent to keep the lifestyle you enjoy or preventing you from having while owning a home. Account for expenses you currently have, ones that the lender doesn't know about, and ones you believe you might have in the future. For example, if you know you plan to start a family, it makes sense to plug in what daycare cost will look like for you when that expense becomes a reality. Include amounts you put into short-term savings and retirement accounts. They should not be optional in your calculations.

When you adapt the GDS/TDS into NGDS/NTDS, you will have a quick picture of your true housing cost and whether you will end up being house poor. The ratios also should provide you a quick starting point to have a more in-depth conversation around your mortgage debt and what it translates into in terms of the lifestyle you and your loved ones will have.

Let's run an example to get you comfortable with how to calculate the ratios.

Lagos recently got married to his wife Osaka. They both are working professionals and are looking to purchase their first home. They found a townhouse in an area they really like. The house is listed for $500,000 and they plan to put down 5% savings from their Retirement Savings Plan (RRSP). Lagos earns $60,000 yearly as an Area Sales Representative for a financing company. Osaka works as a lawyer for a local firm and earns $120,000 per year. For this example, I'm just going to assume they reside and work in Manitoba, a province in Canada.

I'm assuming those amounts constitute the only income Lagos and Osaka receive, and to keep this example simple, the amounts are just straight income from their employer with no deductions other than required taxes deducted by their employer. I calculated their net income using the Canada Revenue Agency (CRA) payroll calculator as of 2021, which is found on the CRA website. Lagos's net monthly income will be $3,644.47; Osaka's monthly net income is $6,349.09.

The property they are looking to purchase requires the following:

- → Property tax of $291 per month
- → Property insurance of $200 per month

→ Estimated water/garbage of $100 per month

→ Estimated heating cost of $95 per month

→ Joint car loan for $250 per month

→ Strata fee of $250 per month

They have no other debt obligations reported by the credit bureau.

Their mortgage application has been approved with a monthly payment $2,337.83 (includes mortgage insurance premium) based on 5% down payment. They have selected a five-year fixed rate at 3% with 25-year amortization.

Their lender's GDS works out to be 18.99%, while their TDS is 20.66%. Those are pretty good ratios if you ask me, and it sounds like they are buying shelter, not mortgage poverty. However, remember the lender uses their gross income to get their respective GDS/TDS. As such, the lender is using a gross monthly income of $5,000 for Lagos and gross monthly income of $10,000 for Osaka. Now, let's calculate their NGDS/NTDS to see how different the numbers are compared to the lender's ratios.

GDS

$$\frac{\$2,337.83 + \$291 + \$125 + \$95}{\$15,000}$$

$$= 18.99\%$$

TDS

$$\frac{\$2,337.83 + \$291 + \$125 + \$95 + 250}{\$15,000}$$

$$= 20.66\%$$

To calculate their NGDS and NTDS I will use the exact same income provided earlier for both of them and keep all the expenses the same. The only change is using Lagos and Osaka's net take home pay after taxes, which is $3,644.47 per month for Lagos and $6,349.09 per month for Osaka for total combined income of $9,993.56. Based on that information, their NGDS will be 32.76%, while their NTDS will be 35.26%. This is why homeowners often feel stretched and cannot do anything but pay their mortgage. The lender's GDS/TDS is beneficial to the lender's business as it ensures continued approval of mortgage loans. The NGDS/NTDS gives you a quick way to clearly see a more accurate cost of your home.

NGDS

$$\frac{\$2{,}337.83 + \$291 + \$250 + \$95 + 100 + 200}{\$9{,}993.56}$$

$$= 32.76\%$$

NTDS

$$\frac{\$2{,}337.83 + \$291 + \$250 + \$95 + \$100 + \$200 + \$250}{\$9{,}993.56}$$

$$= 35.26\%$$

In doing so, you can easily see that while the lender is showing Osaka and Lagos's housing cost as only 18.99% of their combined gross income, their actual housing cost is almost 33% of their net pay. True, that percent is still good, but not as good as what the lender is seeing on their side. Lenders are not looking at an applicant's entire picture but are selecting only expenses they wish to acknowledge to approve the loan. Osaka and Lagos's higher NGDS and NTDS percents include home insurance and city water/garbage cost.

The example illustrates that simply because you are approved for a mortgage doesn't mean the lender is saying you can afford the mortgage. Only you can make that determination, and the adjustment to the GDS/TDS formula will give you a quick way to see a home's true affordability. Remember, the key is basing your mortgage obligation on your net pay and other real-life expenses in order to maintain the lifestyle you want. You have to do the difficult homework to see if the mortgage being offered is actually one you can afford and what the true cost of your home actually is.

CHAPTER 19

MORTGAGE PAYMENT ISN'T ABOUT CONVENIENCE

C anadian household debt stood at 177% of disposable income in 2019, which is up from 168% in 2018.[67] The statistic means that for every $1 in disposable income, they owed $1.77 in debt. The biggest debt that Canadians owe is mortgage debt, which makes up roughly 40% of all debts.[68] Yet, in the 2021 Mortgage Consumer Survey Results, 41% of respondents had a monthly mortgage payment with the second most popular mortgage payment option being biweekly at 26%.[69] It's surprising to see monthly and bi-weekly as the most popular mortgage payment option selected,

---

67 "Canadians and their Money: Key Findings from the 2019 Canadian Financial Capability Survey," Government of Canada, updated April 29, 2020, https://www.canada.ca/en/financial-consumer-agency/programs/research/canadian-financial-capability-survey-2019.html.

68 Ibid.

69 "Mortgage Consumer Survey Results Are in!" CMHC online, March 31, 2021, https://www.cmhc-schl.gc.ca/en/professionals/housing-markets-data-and-research/housing-research/surveys/mortgage-consumer-surveys/survey-results-2021.

since these are the least effective payment options for paying off your mortgage debt sooner.[70]

I've yet to meet someone who likes having a mortgage. I've met people who like having a home but never met a person who said, "I love having to make mortgage payments." The difference in paying off your mortgage earlier could come down to what type of mortgage payment option you selected. Most financial concepts are simple, and their simplicity is often why people don't follow them. They can't believe it's that simple. The simplest way to ensure you pay off your mortgage is first selecting the right type of mortgage payment option. Here's why. Mortgage interest is not calculated in advance, and the compounding period for mortgages are semi-annually in Canada. What does that mean for you? It means frequency and additional payments are critical to cutting years off your mortgage and saving on interest cost.

MORTGAGE PAYMENT OPTIONS AVAILABLE IN CANADA

There are six mortgage payment options offered by most Canadian lenders. You can pay your mortgage payments monthly, semi-monthly, bi-weekly, weekly, accelerated bi-weekly, accelerated weekly. Most people, when deciding on which payment option they will go with, make their decision based on convenience. Homeowners will simply pick a payment option that matches up with their pay cycle or what's convenient for them.

If a homeowner is seeking to pay off their mortgage in the quickest possible time, there are only two mortgage payment options you should ever consider. They are accelerated bi-weekly and accelerated weekly payments. That's it! Except for doubling up payments to the other

---

70   "Mortgage Payment Options," Ratehub, accessed August 13, 2021, https://www.ratehub.ca/mortgage-payment-options.

options, no other payment option makes sense unless you have some weird love with making mortgage payments.

I should end this chapter there, but the practice bothers me so much I've ensured the next few pages will be dedicated to explaining why it makes no sense for lenders to even offer the other four payment types if lenders truly want to assist homeowners in paying off their mortgage as soon as possible.

The frequency of your payment along with additional payments are critical to cutting years off your mortgage and saving on interest cost. Additional and more frequent payments reduce your amortization year, which essentially forces the extra payment to pay off your mortgage quicker. But that's a lot to do when you've taken on an $800,000 mortgage that will already have a high monthly payment. That's why you should focus first on doing the obvious and simple thing by setting up the right payment option that will help you pay off your mortgage faster without stretching you thin.

WHAT'S THE DIFFERENCE BETWEEN BIWEEKLY AND ACCELER-ATED BIWEEKLY?

I got into an argument with someone once about why biweekly payments do little to nothing for paying down their mortgage or reducing their amortization when compared to monthly payments. They got mad at me and said something to the effect that I was wrong, and that they make an extra mortgage payment since their payment is on a biweekly frequency.

To counter them, I asked them a few questions to prove my point. First, I asked the person what their annual salary was? They didn't want to share. I said no problem, let's just work with a hypothetical example.

I asked him to assume that he got paid $40,000 per year and that he chooses to be paid biweekly. He said, okay. I said that would work out to 26 payments in a year, correct? He agreed. I followed up and said that schedule will usually work out to two or three paychecks per month depending on the month, correct? He nodded. I asked him, so in a year, how much were you paid? He paused, I smiled, and he walked away. By the way, the answer is still $40,000! Just because you are paid in a certain frequency doesn't mean your employer pays you more at the end of the year.

Mortgage payments work the same. If you take out a mortgage where the total interest and principal payment you have to make per year comes to $40,000, and you decide to make that payment over 26 biweekly payment, it's still $40,000. You could have done it over 12 months, but you wanted to do it over 26 payments because it matched your pay frequency. But what you paid at the end of year still doesn't change, which is $40,000. That outcome is why biweekly and monthly payments are more or less the same type of payment, with biweekly payments often selected by homeowners because they match with their salary pay frequency.

The only mortgage payment option you should pick is either accelerated bi-weekly or accelerated weekly. Anything else is pretty much saying you love having a mortgage and nothing makes you happier than making mortgage payments. And if that truly is the case, select monthly, by all means.

But why are accelerated bi-weekly and bi-weekly payments different? They both have bi-weekly in their name; therefore, how different are they? A small difference between these two payment types can make a huge impact on your mortgage debt. Let me explain the payment options in more detail.

Accelerated bi-weekly payments are calculated differently than biweekly payments. To calculate an accelerated bi-weekly payment, you take equivalent monthly mortgage payment and divide that amount by two and make 26 equal payments throughout the year. The result is that you make payments more frequently and end up making an extra mortgage payment compared to a monthly or biweekly payment schedule. By following the accelerated bi-weekly schedule, you save not only on total interest but also reduce several years off your mortgage term, as shown in the following table.

Let's assume you want to purchase a home for $400,000 with 5% as down payment. You've secured a five-year mortgage term at a fixed rate of 3% with a 25-year amortization. The chart below shows all the various payment options available and the impact they would have on the overall mortgage cost. I've also assumed a total mortgage loan of $395,200 that includes the mortgage insurance premium.

PAYMENT FREQUENCY	MONTHLY	SEMI-MONTHLY
Payment Amount	$1,870.27	$934.74
Amortization	25 years	25 years
Total Interest Paid	**$165,879.86**	**$165,645.57**
Total Interest Savings Compared to Monthly Payment	$0.00	$234.29
Number of Years Eliminated	None	None

BI-WEEKLY	WEEKLY	ACCELERATED BI-WEEKLY	ACCELERATED WEEKLY
$862.81	$431.32	$935.13	$467.57
25 years	25 years	25 years	25 years
$165,627.55	**$165,519.38**	**$145,499.65**	**$145,279.22**
$252.32	$360.48	$20,380.22	$20,600.64
None	None	2 years and 8 months*	2 years and 9 months*

Approximately

A monthly payment option is the least effective way to pay off your mortgage sooner and save interest cost. The amortization remains at 25 years, and it has the highest total interest of all the options over the 25 years of the loan. Semi-monthly is a little better on interest savings, but the mortgage doesn't get paid earlier. Bi-weekly and weekly payments get better as more frequent payments are being made, which results in greater interest savings compared to monthly payments; however, it still takes 25 years to pay off the mortgage.

But look at the accelerated bi-weekly and accelerated weekly payment option. The person who takes either has no interest in making mortgage payments and wants the mortgage paid off as quickly as possible. Compared to monthly, the accelerated bi-weekly payment option results in paying off the mortgage almost three years earlier. The total interest savings over the 25-year period amounts to $20,380.22 for accelerated bi-weekly compared to only $252.32 on the bi-weekly payment option. But that's not the big deal. The really big deal is the minimal cost difference of only $72.32 bi-weekly ($935.13-$862.81) between opting for an accelerated bi-weekly payment compared to the bi-weekly payment. For only an extra $72.32 bi-weekly (just $6 extra per day), you could have your mortgage paid off almost three years earlier.

Please do not pick any other mortgage payment option that isn't accelerated bi-weekly or accelerated weekly (assuming you can juggle the respective amounts each week or every two weeks). No one enjoys making mortgage payments. You like your home, and you like spending time with your family and friends at home, but you don't like making mortgage payments. You shouldn't want to pay your mortgage for an extra three years simply because it matches up with your pay cycle.

CHAPTER 20

NOW YOU KNOW WHAT THE BANKS DON'T TELL YOU

This concludes Part 2 of the book. Congratulations on reading through this part as you should now have a basic understanding of the mortgage approval process. Don't worry if you didn't get it all initially on first read. Re-read and reference again and again.

The information provided was not written to make you a mortgage underwriter. It was written to increase your knowledge concerning mortgage qualification to help you better understand how and why you get approved for a mortgage. The knowledge will assist you in being able to have a more in-depth conversation on mortgages with the individual or institution you choose to secure your mortgage.

As a result of reading this book, you now know that to qualify for a mortgage you need to meet certain mortgage ratios known as gross debt service (GDS) and total debt service ratio (TDS). You also now know how lenders calculate these ratios and the specific maximum you have to be within to get an approval. Therefore, if a lender advises you that they declined your application as your GDS was out of line, you now know what it means.

You also now know what mortgage insurance is. You know that a high-ratio mortgage is one in which the lender purchases mortgage insurance on the loan to cover the potential of your defaulting on the loan. Mortgage insurance is good for the lender and also helps you as you don't have to put as large of a down payment under a high-ratio mortgage. You also now know that you pay the premium for the mortgage insurance coverage with all the benefits going to the lender in the event of a loan loss.

If your mortgage application is declined due to your overall credit score or profile, you now know the information that makes up your credit score and how you can improve your credit score. If your application was declined due to your income level, you now have a rough idea of how lenders calculate the most often used income in mortgage applications along with the type of documents they might request from you.

But the most important thing you've now learned in reading this section is that lenders approve your mortgage loan based on your gross income and expect you to make payments based on your after-tax net income. Due to that method and from information gathered in this book, you now know that the mortgage loan you are approved for is based on an income level that you do not actually take home. Therefore, it's crucial that you be the one to determine the right amount of mortgage loan debt you want to take on and not simply assume that the lender's approval is the same thing as saying you can afford the loan.

To avoid getting a loan that you can't afford, you now know you need to figure out the total housing cost for the home you wish to purchase. You also now have a quick formula in the Net Gross Debt Service (NGDS) and Net Total Debt Service (NTDS) ratio to see a more complete account of the cost of your home. Therefore, before you even seek a mortgage, you can now determine roughly what your total housing cost will be and the quality of life you can afford with the mortgage debt you acquire.

You also now know things that can add to your mortgage debt, such as frequent refinancing, and that either accelerated bi-weekly payment or accelerated weekly payment will ensure you pay off your mortgage as quickly as possible.

You've learned a lot, and now you can be more confident in talking about your mortgage debt with the professional who will assist you in securing your mortgage. If you would like to work directly with me on your mortgage planning needs, please visit www.wealthmarathon.com to set up a free mortgage consultation. Remember, the goal isn't to become the expert in mortgages but rather to use your increased knowledge level to be able to ask the right set of questions to secure the right amount of mortgage debt for your situation. Applying that wisdom will enable you to live the life you want today while also allowing you to invest in your future.

But to really take things to the next level, you also need to understand some basic financial foundation concepts that when combined with your newly acquired mortgage knowledge will further enable you to build a path toward financial freedom. That's what Part 3 is all about. In the next section, you will learn some basic financial concepts that I have learned over the years that will help you and those you care about to live a more purposeful and financially secure life.

Part 3

Life and Wealth

The biggest fears we face in life are often those created by other human beings.

CHAPTER 21

YOUR FEARS WILL PREVENT YOUR GROWTH

Fear can be a great motivator, or it can paralyze you. Our fears can help us avoid situations that can cause us real harm. That's not the type of fear I want to discuss. The fear I wish to discuss is the one we all struggle with. It's the fear of failure that keeps us from moving forward or causes us to avoid potential things that could enrich our life's journey.

One of my earliest real estate failures was after we completed our basement suite renovation. I was excited to finally have the suite completed and ready to rent it out to someone. At the time, all I was focused on was getting the place rented to be able to refinance our renovation cost into the mortgage loan. I had financed our renovation cost with a one-year low interest credit card that charged 0.99% for the year with a small one-time fee to access the funds. While it was a low interest rate, it was only guaranteed for the year, and after the year was up, the rate would jump to 21%. The renovation already took almost a year to complete, which was much longer than I had anticipated. I felt pressure to get this loan refinanced into our mortgage to avoid having to make a large monthly credit card payment at an extremely high interest rate.

I started the rental search once the suite was ready as I knew the bank would use the rental income to qualify us. However, for the bank to actually use the income, I had to have a renter in place. I put up an online ad for the unit, and after several people came to the view the place, I settled on two prospective tenants who were friends. At the time, I made sure they were working, which they were. I even got a copy of their paystubs to confirm. They were young and hadn't rented a basement suite before. At the time, that situation wasn't much of a concern to me because they both seemed likable and respectful individuals. While there were some concerns that crossed my mind, I didn't follow up on them as the individuals seemed very nice. They mentioned they were friends but had only known each other for a short time and that they met at their local church. I recall thinking, Do they know that living with someone is different than seeing someone every day? But I continued on as my primary concerns were met.

Another sign of concern came at the time of signing the contract and payment of the rent deposit. I had told them they needed to put down half the month's rent as deposit. They advised they would have it on a particular day that we agreed to, but when I called to see if they were coming with the deposit, they advised me they had gone out of town with some other friends and would provide the deposit upon their return. Again, more warning signs crossed my mind. I thought, Why would they not give the deposit before they went on their trip? But I proceeded as I figured everything would just work itself out. I was just happy that I had found someone to rent our place.

Once they moved in, more troubling signs started to show up. Parking become a problem as they parked their vehicle on the street in the opposite direction of the flow of traffic, which caused my neighbors to complain. I explained to the tenants that they should park with the flow of traffic. They accepted my suggestion and assured me it wouldn't happen again, but it happened again, again, and again. After a while, I just gave up and hoped my neighbors wouldn't complain to me.

Rent payment also became an issue as one person would pay me half the rent and then I would have to contact or chase the other person for the remaining rent. I thought to myself, What have I signed my wife and me up for? We are sharing our space with individuals who were not respecting our agreement! I felt like such an idiot as months went on, and I started to reflect on all the warning signs that I failed to listen to. I couldn't believe I didn't investigate all the red flags I saw. In my hurry to rent out the place, I had no process to accomplish what I wanted, and instead I developed tunnel vision, which resulted in my selecting the wrong tenants for our home. It wasn't the tenants' fault as I'm the one who selected them.

They eventually gave me their notice to leave, which I was happy to facilitate because at the time, I didn't really know how to tell them the rental arrangement wasn't working for us. Their reason was that their personal relationship had broken down and because one of the individuals wasn't able to pay the rent on their own.

That outcome is typically why most homeowners do not rent suites within the same home where they are living. If the arrangement goes bad, the consequences can go beyond just the damage of the home but can also cause family frustration. For me, I was fortunate because no major damage was created by them. I don't believe at all that they were bad people but rather that they hadn't ever rented their own space. Renting a basement suite requires both parties to respect each other as they are sharing a common space. I believe their lack of respect was what caused the issues I had with them. But ultimately it was my poor screening process—or lack of one—that put them and me in that position.

My desire to refinance the renovation cost quickly caused me to disregard all the signs indicating that perhaps they were not a good fit for our home. I won't say it was a judgment call about them, but rather where we were in life and where they were in life that didn't make for a good fit, given the space was to be shared between us. I felt bad and wanted to give them a chance because when you're young, it's difficult to secure a rental space. Some landlords will avoid renting to young people because they believe they will party and trash their place. But that assumption is unfair as not all young people will automatically throw a party where they live. The tenants I rented to had moved out of their parents' homes and didn't appreciate that they were sharing a space with another family, and even though it was separated, it was still within one house. The biggest problem wasn't that they were young, but rather they hadn't rented before and weren't familiar with sharing a common space with someone else.

While the experience on the surface appears to be a failure, it actually helped both the tenants and me. It made them better tenants in that I provided the environment for them to fail, which enabled them to practice and experience what it's like to rent a shared place. Their failure also helped me become a better landlord by understanding the need for a better process and system to find individuals who fit the type of space I am seeking to rent.

I don't believe there are such things as failure in life. The only failure you have in life is when you accept that any failure isn't a growth opportunity. My first tenants went on to rent another place, and I'm sure they became excellent tenants for their next landlord. I'm sure they learned a lot through the experience they had with me. I continued on with trying to be a better landlord, though I would have more failures until I finally had some successes.

Fear of failure is a restriction. Our fears and particularly our fear of failure hold us back from personal growth. You can't reach your full potential if you allow your fears or failures to prevent you from trying again. You must find a way to move forward. We learn through our failures, which enable our personal growth through reflection and correction from those experiences.

My first rental failure gave me so much experience and has helped me become a better landlord today. I had to develop systems to help me find the right people who fit the tenant characteristics I was seeking. Today, I ask the right set of questions and don't miss warning signals as much.

Financial success has less to do with your arithmetic skills. Most of us know one plus one equals two. But in the real world, people struggle with their emotions and biases, which can create a situation where they believe one plus one can equal three. It's what makes us human, and predictably, terrible with money.

CHAPTER 22

THE MINDSET FOR WEALTH

A fter I finished playing college basketball, I was seeking out an activity that would be as competitive but was not teamed-based. I always wanted to be on the school track team, so I decided to pick up running. I wanted to do a triathlon but decided against it because I couldn't swim. I finally decided to run a half-marathon, which seemed to fit the bill. I've now run several half-marathons and enjoy the challenge that comes with them. Running a half-marathon well requires a lot of discipline, and when I first started, I had none. I was a former athlete and still had my athlete's ego. I thought, how hard is it to run 21km? It turned out to be pretty hard if you don't keep to your training plan. On my first race, as soon as the race started, I forgot my plan and tried to show off to impress other racers whom I didn't even know.

My poor execution would result in my finishing well past the time I wanted. To make matters worse, when I crossed the finish line, I looked like I had just run a full marathon. But something odd also happened when I crossed the finish line. All the racers who had passed me and whom I didn't know congratulated me. It wasn't unique to me as they were doing the same for other racers as well. In that moment, I realized I had lost perspective on why I even signed up for the race in the first place. I signed up because I wanted something that would be challenging like when I played basketball and to keep me active. But on race day, I forgot all that and focused on my ego.

The racers who stood at the finish line after completing the race understood it didn't matter when a person finished. It just mattered that they did. Some people were faster and more in shape than others, but ultimately, we all just wanted to finish the race.

Running a marathon is a lot like trying to create wealth. People make the same mistake about money and wealth creation that I did on my first half-marathon. They view wealth as a sprint, instead of a marathon. Most of us do try to attain wealth at a pace that isn't based on our unique skills and abilities, as we wish to complete the race quickly. In doing so, similar to running a marathon outside your body's abilities and skills, it often results in an injury. In the money world, that analogy just means you start to have money troubles and never really obtain wealth.

It's an uncomfortable truth, but you can't rush the wealth process. However, most of us are impatient with our wealth journey. We want wealth now but often are not prepared to put in the necessary work or sacrifice required to reach our wealth goal. Instead, we look for quick wealth tricks. We seek short cuts that often result in a lot of pain because we are uncomfortable at obtaining wealth at a pace reflective of our skills and abilities.

As you get older, you come to realize that you can't rush a good thing as you have to be prepared to play the long game. The goal isn't to impress your friends or family but rather to complete the race at a pace that can be maintained for the long run. It's not a sprint, and you need to prepare your mind and body for the long wealth marathon you are about to embark on.

If you are prepared to approach your wealth journey with a marathon mindset, not only are you likely to increase your chance of success, but you will enjoy the journey far more. While the journey will be more enjoyable with a marathon mindset, that attitude doesn't mean you will not have any challenges. You will have a lot of challenges and setbacks along your journey. You have to be prepared to do things differently than others. You have to be prepared to be laughed at for decisions that go against the crowd consensus. You will have to increase your knowledge and train your mind toward constantly learning new things about wealth and accept that the only constant in wealth creation is change. But above all, you must learn to be disciplined with your plan and execute it.

I define being wealthy or financially independent as being able to do what you want with your time. It's not a dollar amount that I use. An individual making $40,000 can be wealthy if they have the freedom to do as they please with their time. Some individuals might feel they need $2 million a year to be able to do what they want with their time. Therefore, when I say wealth, I don't mean a specific number but rather the freedom to do what you enjoy when you want. In fact, wealth and being financially independent are the same to thing to me. Being financially independent is seen as a more noble way of saying wealth, in that saying you're wealthy tends to be viewed as showing off. Those two terms are the same to me, but people typically pick one that feels more in tune with their personality. If you're financially independent, then you're also wealthy. But being rich isn't the same thing as being wealthy or financially independent. One can be rich but not be free to do as they want with their time. You want to work toward being wealthy or financially independent, whichever term you prefer.

If the concepts I share about wealth creation seem obvious to you, then ask yourself if you are applying them. If you are not, then you do not understand the concept yet, but only are aware of the concept or idea. Since wealth isn't just about money, some of the concepts I discuss are not necessarily just about money, but all will tie into wealth creation. I have listed them with a number to make each concept easier to read and for you to quickly locate a concept by its number, but each number does not reflect the importance of one over the other. These concepts aren't about getting rich, but rather about how to create financial independence for you and those you care about. Therefore, I will not be discussing what stocks to buy, but I will instead discuss the concept of investing in the stock market.

Lastly, remember that wealth is a marathon and there are no shortcuts, although many people will offer you shortcuts at your expense. I believe the concepts I offer will help you along your financial independence journey, but I cannot walk the path for you. Therefore, use them to assist in creating your own unique wealth plan that can help you finish the wealth marathon. At the end of the day, you want to cross the finish line as it's the experiences you have on your wealth journey that make them worth pursuing, not the asset or income streams you might accumulate along the way.

CHAPTER 23

WEALTH THAT LASTS

1. Pay yourself first and invest in yourself always

The concept of paying yourself first is one that most people in principle understand but behaviorally struggle to implement. Most of us understand that our money should be working for us, but our budgets don't reflect that. If you're going to achieve wealth, your behavior must be in accordance with the concept.

Most of the income we earn is often used to create wealth for others in return for short-term emotional satisfaction. As such, many people's budgets consist of items that they pay for to help them feel good in the short term but prevent them from being able to make long-term investments for themselves. We've conditioned ourselves to accept that wealth or anything worthwhile must come now rather than understanding it's a process and there are no shortcuts to success.

That being the case, it's essential that you start making investments in yourself and the things that truly bring you happiness. When you get paid, you need to ensure the first payee on your list is you. Yes, you come before your mortgage, car payment, and any other bills. If you don't make yourself a priority, then you will continue to pay other people and continue to move yourself to the bottom of the payee list. The effect of such behavior is like saying your mortgage is more important than paying yourself. Of course, paying your mortgage is important. It's just not more important than paying yourself first. If you don't make the necessary investment in yourself, you will continue to pay someone else an income stream in the form of your mortgage payment because you fail to make yourself the most important payee.

How do you check if you are paying yourself first? Check your budget. How much of your income is going to other people and how much of your income is toward investment in yourself? That's the most basic and simple way to confirm if you are paying yourself first. You want to work toward having a high savings rates and low debt payment. A high savings rates means you are not paying unnecessary expenses (income streams) to other people or businesses. Instead, you are taking those savings and investing the money in yourself.

A low savings rate could be a sign that your money is not working for you but rather works for others.

How well you understand that concept is revealed by your habits. Make the change to ensure you are the first one who gets paid as you are the one who is giving up your precious limited time.

2.   Create and use a budget as a financial accountability tool

Creating accountability is important if you're trying to accomplish anything in life. Personal finance is no different. One of the biggest reasons people struggle with their finances is that they fail to set aside a time to think and plan how they want to spend their money. Perhaps the easiest and simplest way to create financial accountability is to use a monthly budget.

A budget is like a map: It helps you plan an appropriate route to reach your financial goals. While there are many benefits to working with a budget, I want to highlight my top three reasons why you should consider using a budget.

- → **Creates accountability.** You have to first hold yourself accountable if you plan to be successful. Everything starts with you, and it's important to ensure that you're doing all the right things to put yourself in a successful position before you look at other areas or other people.

- → **Helps create good financial habits**. When you work with a budget, you develop financially good habits. You learn to work with a fixed income level, which will help you prepare for the day when you will have to live on a fixed income.

- → **Enables you to plan**. A lot of people do mental planning. The problem with mental planning is that it's easy to forget things. Tracking things in your head makes it too easy to avoid being accountable since nothing is documented. When you create a budget, include what's important to you today and think of what might be important to you tomorrow. Put your thoughts on paper so you can constantly reflect on them. Spend money on items that improve or add to the quality of your life. Also, avoid overspending on things that do not improve the quality of your life.

Failing to create and follow a budget is likely to result in your spending money on things that really don't matter to you. It's a given that most successful companies in the world follow an operating budget. But, as I mentioned before, the results of the 2019 Mortgage Consumer Survey revealed that 33% of all buyers did not have a monthly budget in place before they bought their home.[71]

A budget is critical to have and especially important when shopping for a home to keep you accountable. When you spend the time to make a budget, you start thinking about how best to spend your money to make yourself the happiest. In short, you create a mindset that says, "I pay myself first and not the bills first." Here are four tips to assist you, as well as which expenses to include in your budget. Remember, if you don't write it down, it's easy to let yourself off the hook.

IT'S A BUDGET, NOT A PUNISHMENT

Maybe you hate being restricted and that's why you avoid using a budget. I can understand the feeling as I hate feeling restricted as well. A budget isn't a restriction or a punishment if done right. A budget provides you the time to be thoughtful about the things you want your money to provide for you. Spending however you wish without any thoughtful consideration to your spending eventually leads to feeling restricted and, worse, lowers the quality of life you will have.

Your budget is about you and focusing on what really makes you happy. It's about your taking the time to think about the type of life you want to have. The concept isn't about the money but instead about you as well as the decisions and impact you want to have with your money. It's about the life you want to live today and the legacy you want to leave behind.

Stop with the punishment excuses already and focus on directing your money toward what matters to you.

---

71 "The State of Homebuying in Canada: 2019 CMHC Mortgage Consumer Survey."

MAKE SAVING A NON-NEGOTIABLE AND MANDATORY EXPENSE

When creating a budget, it's often easy to focus on making sure you can pay your bills but forgetting to pay yourself. To avoid that mindset, simply treat saving as an expense within your budget. Focus less on a certain percentage at first, and simply focus on putting away any amount you can each month. If your income varies, adjust the amount of savings up or down accordingly, but always pay yourself something. Make savings non-negotiable and pay it every single month just like your rent/mortgage. By including savings as an expense, you will start to develop the habit of paying yourself first, and once that habit clicks in, putting away 20% of your monthly income or as much as possible will seem like a no-brainer. At that point, the thought of not paying yourself will seem both ridiculous and offensive.

Saving every month increases your future cash flow and ensures that you always pay yourself first.

DETAIL IN TRACKING IS CRITICAL TO SUCCESS

Everything needs to be accounted for in your budget. A successful budget needs to account for all your expenses and spending. Detail is critical to really understand how you're spending your money. A gym membership, eating out, buying personal items, and other similar small expenses have to be accounted for. It's critical to create a picture of how your money is being spent, which will help you change any bad habits you might have.

DISPLAY YOUR BUDGET VISUALLY AS WELL AS A PERCENTAGE TO INCOME

I'm a visual person, so my budget information is done through a spreadsheet with the information converted and displayed in graphs and charts. Each expense is further broken down to percentage of income. I also have a yearly report that shows what was actually spent in the year relative to what I budgeted. Today, you can also use apps such as Mint, which will help you with tracking your budget automatically and displays them visually. Seeing the same information presented in different ways provides a fresh perspective.

For example, you might budget $100 per month for eating out, which on the surface seems reasonable. But if that same $100 translates to 30% of your after-tax income, you might feel differently about the same $100. The amount budgeted hasn't changed; rather, the information has been presented in a different way to provide another perspective. Making good financial decisions requires information to be presented in multiple formats to enable you to see the complete picture of your spending habits.

EVERYTHING IS BETTER WITH A GLASS OF WINE

Okay, so maybe that isn't really a tip, but rather an excuse to add a line about wine in the book. In all seriousness, if you're in a relationship and trying to do a budget, things can get a little intense. So, my advice is to have a glass of wine or your favorite beverage or food. Doing a budget on your own is hard enough; trying to merge two people's ideology on money is harder, but it's not impossible.

If you're a couple, try to have some fun with it. Remember it's not a punishment. It's about both of you taking the time to discuss and plan your future, which should be exciting and not a punishment. Whatever you do, please avoid doing a budget on your own without feedback from your partner. Couples, in my opinion, must take a collaborative approach to their budget to ensure both are represented. If you fail to get the buy-in from your partner, you will find it difficult to reach your goals as your partner will end up becoming an obstacle because they do not feel represented. Don't do that. Include them as it's your collective goals, not only one person's goal and dreams.

3.   Hard work alone will not bring financial success

In today's economic system, you will not succeed if all you do is work hard. It should be obvious, too, that you will not succeed without hard work, but hard work alone will not guarantee your success with money. That's the simple reality of how most economic systems work.

Hard work is what most people believe in, and therefore, most people believe if they work hard then they will eventually be rewarded. If all you do is work hard, then you're likely to die from stretching yourself thin and will only be able to keep up your hard work until your body decides to shut down.

You have to learn to work hard and smart. Most successful people are extremely hard working, but more importantly, they work smart. Wealthy individuals know that if all they do is put in labor hours each day, then eventually they will be broke the day they get injured or eventually burn out.

Therefore, they focus their effort on working smart and hard. Most of their time is spent working on developing systems that initially require a lot of work (labor), but once set up, enable them to not have to put in as much labor hours over time.

If most of your income is used to only take care of your expenses, then you are likely just working hard. Many people spend all their effort just working hard. They might work a ton of overtime, work two jobs, or earn high income in a stressful position. Those situations don't allow you to think of ways to work smarter, and as such, you continue to work hard only.

That path is unsustainable for your body and terrible for your financial well-being. You need to figure out how to work smart and hard by using your time to create systems that don't require as much labor input over time.

Wealthy individuals work hard to create systems that require less and less of their time to maintain but continue to pay them an income stream. That's working smart. Individuals who struggle with money tend to work extremely hard at one system that requires more and more of their labor to maintain over time, which eventually leads to frustration, unhappiness, and most importantly giving up their most valuable asset, which is their time.

4. Information is the real commodity that people trade

In a free market system, the real commodity is knowledge. While people trade silver, gold, and even Bitcoin, what they are really trading is information. The more knowledge you have over the entity you are dealing with, the more profit you will be able to extract from the deal. The lesser the knowledge gap among trading parties, the lower the profit as there's no real advantage each has over the other. Humans want to be fair but often create systems that support the exact opposite.

For example, this book has provided you information that should be standard, in my opinion, but the homebuying system doesn't provide homeowners the right information they require. As such, the system ends up not providing critical information to homeowners, which leads to many of them making costly mistakes when purchasing a home simply because no one gives them the knowledge.

Since the real commodity being traded is knowledge and not physical or digital, you should spend your time and energy understanding financial transactions you get involved in. You especially need to educate yourself on "big ticket" items that have long-term implications, like auto loans and home purchases. The knowledge gap is often large in those who offer the product for sale and those looking to purchase the product. Therefore, educating yourself beforehand is so critical for you to be successful with big-ticket items.

5. Buy, invest, or create income-producing assets

In a market system, inequality is its nature. How much inequity that exists is left to the participants. One of the driving factors for inequity is the accumulation of wealth. In a market system, success isn't the result of those who earn the most income, but rather those who control resource production or capital. Said differently, a person who owns the means to production or capital is more likely to be wealthier over time compared to someone who earns a high salary income. Most people chase high income when they should chase resource/capital accumulation. If you earn a high income but do not own production or capital resources, you will not be wealthy for long, or your wealth will end when your job does.

To avoid such a scenario, you want to buy, invest, or create income-producing assets. If you place your money in one of those areas, you're likely to create lasting wealth. However, as a general rule, buying a principal residence with no income stream doesn't meet that concept. You don't want to just own appreciating assets; rather, you want to own appreciating assets that also produce an income stream. Being asset rich can be poverty in the waiting because it creates the belief you are wealthy because you own an asset of high value, but in reality, you can be poorer because the assets can take up a large percent of your income while not producing any income on their own to offset the debt obligation.

True wealth isn't asset accumulation. It's cash flow accumulation. Assets satisfy people's egos, but cash flow runs their daily lives. That's why the concept has the phrase "income-producing" in it to emphasize cash flow. Income-producing assets are what you want to invest your money in.

You don't want to be rich or asset-rich only. You want to be wealthy, which means you own assets that produce a positive cash flow stream.

6. Learn a little about the psychology of money

One of the radio stations I listen to on my way to work has a contest in which they give listeners a chance to win a large sum of money. The game is fairly straightforward. The lucky listener who is selected, gets to open a set of boxes until they hear the buzzer. Each box they open without a buzzer has a sum of money they can collect if they choose. For example, the caller might open box #1 for $100, box #2 for $150, and box #3 for $200. Assuming the caller decides to stop at box #3, they would be entitled to $200. If the caller instead opted to continue to play another box, in this case box #4, which happens to be the box with the buzzer, then the caller loses everything they might have earned and will be given only a restaurant gift card for $100.

I enjoy listening to the game as it reminds me of how irrational we can be around money. Every caller who plays this game has a pre-determined dollar amount they wish to collect. Based on the number of times I've listened to this game, it appears everyone wants to get to the $1,000 mark. I'm not entirely sure why people want to reach a $1,000, but if a caller reaches it, they typically stop playing any additional boxes. The radio station does something very important if the individual decides to stop before the buzzer comes on. They play out what would have happened had the individual not stopped so early. Usually when this occurs, it's often shown that had the individual played more boxes, then they could have won a big sum of money—not always but usually.

From a rational standpoint, the decision to be made around this game is fairly straightforward when I look at it. Since the callers started with nothing, then they should play until they've reached an amount above what they initially started with before they were selected for the game. Any amount before the buzzer looks like success. However, the callers actually didn't start at $0 because the radio station offered a $100 restaurant card regardless of the result. Therefore, the participant's actual starting floor is $100, not $0. As such, anything above $100 is a really good rational point to exit and end the game. That's the rational way to play it.

However, that's not how people play this game. Irrationality is easy to see in other people's behavior but harder to see in your own. People struggle with money largely because they simply do not appreciate or understand how irrational they truly are or can be around money or life in general. They often don't put proper systems and measures in place to stop or help them identify their irrationality, which often creates money problems for them. A good example is those who sign up for gym memberships but continue to renew it even after they stop going, hoping one day to use it again.

You have to understand that money has a weird psychological effect on your brain, and each of us has unique as well as common psychological money biases that will prevent us from making good money decisions. To assist with that condition, here are six common money biases you should be aware of that might contribute to your being irrational with money.

LOSS AVERSION

This bias is the reason you will hang on to things that are no longer profitable. For example, you might own a stock, which you've lost money on but have no prospect of recovering from your loss position. However, due to actual or imagined pain you might feel by selling the stock, you would rather hold on to the stock even at a loss than to sell the stock and have to realize the loss, thanks to loss aversion. You will feel more pain from losing money than the joy you feel when you make money. It's important to be aware that you might be holding onto things or avoiding selling financial assets in an effort to avoid feeling the pain of financial loss.[72]

---

72 "Behavioural insights: key concepts, applications and regulatory considerations," Ontario Securities Commission, accessed August 13, 2021, https://www.getsmarteraboutmoney.ca/resources/publications/research/behavioural-insights-key-concepts-applications-regulatory-considerations/.

FRAMING

Any good salesperson will use framing and may not even know they are. Framing is understanding that people are always looking to simplify their decision-making process, and the way information is presented becomes important. Let's see how it works with an example.

Which yogurt would you buy?

> Yogurt A
>
> $9.99 and is 99% fat free.
>
> Yogurt B
>
> $9.99 and only has 1% fat.

Framing is understanding that you might pick a certain option depending on how the information is communicated to you. Some might be more likely to buy yogurt A as it says it's 99% fat free, while some might pick yogurt B as it only has 1% fat. Both products are the same, but the manner in which the information is communicated to you might result in your choosing one over the other.

Framing is huge in the real estate industry. Every communication you get from a realtor or read about a listing is likely being framed in a manner to keep your focus on the positive features of the home only. A recent trend that I have seen in listing descriptions is the mention of a home being a potential development opportunity. The wording of the listing is designed to frame the value of the home to be about the development potential rather than the actual current state of the property, which in the listings I've seen, tend to be properties that require renovation. The conversation of value is no longer about the current state of the property but rather its future potential.

Be careful with framing, especially on your home search. Do your pre-work before reading listings or going on your search to avoid being framed into a purchase that doesn't fit your needs.[73]

CHOICE OVERLOAD

Most of us feel overwhelmed when we are given multiple options. The more options we are given the greater the likelihood we will be unable to make a decision, and even if we do make a decision, it will not be well thought-out.

As decisions get more complex, we tend to just want to stop the process and pick whatever option will end it. It's why homeownership is difficult for a lot of people. They have a lot of options to consider. Is a condo better than a detached home? Which mortgage is better, open or closed term? Should you go with a variable- or fixed-rate mortgage? On and on it goes. Due to its being such an emotional and complex purchase, most people just want to get through the process. The array of information is too much, and as a result most people tend to make a decision that will get them through the process quickly rather than making the right decision that will be good for them.[74]

FAMILIARITY BIAS

Familiarity bias speaks to the notion that most of us tend to do things we are familiar with. We tend to invest in the companies we know and trust.[75] It isn't a bad thing to trust what you are familiar with; however, it can create real money problems. For example, when I worked at the bank, there was a tendency for clients' equity investment portfolio to be heavy in Canadian stock. I tried to explain to clients that they needed

73   Ibid.

74   Ibid.

75   "Familiarity bias," Ontario Securities Commission, accessed August 13, 2021, https://www.getsmarteraboutmoney.ca/resources/publications/research/behavioural-insights-key-concepts-applications-regulatory-considerations/familiarity-bias/.

to diversify their investment holdings by reducing their Canadian stocks and buying more non-Canadian stock as Canada only made up approximately 2.4% of the total world equity market. Having a portfolio that's overweighted in Canadian stocks meant my clients were only able to access 2.4% of the world's total equity return.[76]

Canadian investors are comfortable with buying all Canadian stocks because they are familiar with Canadian companies. They live in Canada, and therefore it appears logical to own Canadian stocks. However, such familiarity bias will certainly cost Canadian investors.

HERD BEHAVIOR

As humans, we can behave like a pack of running buffaloes when one buffalo starts moving and the others just follow. Following the herd can make you a lot of money if you understand that it's something human beings (including me) cannot refuse at times. We all want to be part of a group or be accepted into a group. But before you follow, you should at least ask yourself why you're following.

To understand herd behavior is to recognize that sometimes what you think is happening isn't really what is happening, but often a result of the effect of people around you and your desire to fit in or be accepted by them. Our behavior most of the time is wired to please the groups we want to be part of. That tendency can be dangerous, as it feels good to be part of a group and it's hard to leave the protection of the group. Therefore, the best way to avoid herd bias is to be aware of it and also learn to start thinking thoughtfully about and analyzing your own behavior and others'. It might be a good idea to run with the group, but you have to be able to first determine that truth for yourself and then run with it if that's the right thing.[77]

---

76 "Credit Suisse Global Investment Returns Yearbook 2021 Summary Edition," Credit Suisse, March 2021.

77 "Behavioural insights: key concepts, applications and regulatory considerations."

OVERCONFIDENCE

During the initial outbreak of COVID-19, CMHC released a report in which they advised that house prices would drop significantly.[78] They got a lot of flak about the report as the opposite happened. The market shot up and prices increased. Overconfidence can be a tricky one for all of us. It's one of the reasons that I tend to end talks about money with "but I could be completely wrong." The CMHC report on the housing market during the height of COVID-19 wasn't wrong or illogical. What CMHC failed to appreciate is that economy in the real world isn't based on rationality. How people will behave to economic distress can be extremely difficult to predict, but it's safe to say it will likely be irrational.

Overconfidence can be attributed to some people's failure to plan for retirement because they have a great job with a defined benefit pension plan. They never consider what would happen if they got injured and do not make it to retirement to collect their full pension. At my time at the bank, most clients never even considered such a possibility, or others like divorce, and when such unforeseen events occurred—especially later in their life—well, that pension didn't seem as safe anymore as it once looked. Most of us have far too much confidence in how the future will play out, when, in reality, we have no control, and no one knows.

It's why no matter how sure you are about anything with money or life, you should always ask yourself, "But what if I'm wrong?" Best to create a plan to address the possibility or even the likelihood of your being wrong. If you can accept that you might be wrong even when all signs point to not a chance of it occurring, then at least if the worst happens, you're likely not to lose as much. You should be confident in life but not so confident that you think you can predict the future.

---

78 "Housing market will feel effect of COVID-19 until 2022, CMHC says," CBC, updated May 28, 2020, https://www.cbc.ca/news/business/chmc-housing-report-1.5586732.

The psychology of money might at first not seem connected to wealth, mortgages, or even homeownership, but they are. The appreciation of the complexity of your psychological tendency regarding money and how that tendency can produce habits and behavior that can often be detrimental to your financial and emotional well-being is important to learn and understand. Learning about such tendencies will help you better understand yourself while also reducing the effects they might have. Purchasing a home is an emotional purchase, and the high emotionality around it is what makes it easy not to pay attention to the debt, as after all our homes often serve more than just a place to call home. Therefore, I recommend three books that will reduce your knowledge gap in the psychology of money by helping you appreciate the complexity of how we make decisions.

First, I recommend you start with Influence: *The Psychology of Persuasion* by Robert B. Cialdini, Ph.D. It is a great book to start with if you're a first-time homebuyer or even a repeat buyer. The book will provide insight into influence others might utilize in trying to sell you a home, which will be of extreme value to you during your homeownership journey.[79] The second book I recommend is *Predictably Irrational: The Hidden Forces That Shape Our Decisions* by Dr. Dan Ariely. This book really opened my mind to how what we often think isn't often what we think it is, but rather influenced by others. Similar to the first book, it will further assist your being able to see such influences being used or how they can be impacting your decision-making process.[80] The final book is *How to Lie with Statistics* by Darrell Huff. This book will help you understand why defining what average means is important before accepting such a statistic, which can influence your purchasing decision.[81] These three books will

79   Robert B. Cialdini, *Influence: The Psychology of Persuasion* (New York, NY: HarperBusiness, 2006).

80   Dan Ariely, *Predictably Irrational: The Hidden Forces That Shape Our Decisions* (New York, NY: Harper Perennial, 2010).

81   Darrell Huff, *How to Lie with Statistics* (New York, NY: W. W. Norton & Company, 1993).

give you a better appreciation on the psychology of our behavior, which in turn will help you slow down the homeownership process to allow your rational brain to be able to assess the information being presented to you. With understanding, you can make a more informed decision with fewer influences driving your decision.

7. Build your incorporated business

One of the challenges I have with traditional work is the mindset it tends to create. Our careers and things we do are not who we are or a reflection of what we are capable of. Each of us is capable of much more than just our work, and often when we work, we start to create a mindset of dependency on our employer. Furthermore, we can start to believe our work is all we are capable of.

When you develop a mindset in which you start to depend on your employer to provide for you, rather than understanding that you are the business and your employer is just a client, it's no wonder you start to believe the $60,000 you earn through your employer is actually your marketplace worth. That's why most people fight hard for a 1% yearly salary increase when it might not even cover the annual inflation increase. Oddly enough, your employer views you as a client. The term client isn't bad. You could be an extremely valuable client of your employer, which is what you should work toward, but you still shouldn't depend on your employer to provide everything you need.

Instead of having the dependency mindset, you need to start building what I call the "YOU.Incorporated" business. I want you to start thinking of yourself as a business with multiple lines of businesses. You need to shift your mindset from expecting people to provide for you to fully understanding you are the business.

Your employer wants to do business with you. You are not working for them. It's good for both you and your employer to have that mindset as that's the reality of your contract with each other. The traditional mindset of employees is seeking to simply do enough to not get fired. The YOU. Incorporated individual understands the work they do is a reflection on their employer's business and wants to maximize the business return by doing excellent work, for which they rightfully expect to be compensated appropriately. In short, YOU.Incorporated individuals aren't concerned about being fired but rather seek a client (employer) who sees their value in delivering excellent work to drive the employer's business skills and talents and their own, and as such, the employer (client) is more than willing to compensate such individuals appropriately for their value.

The graph below illustrates how I want you to think about your YOU. Incorporated business. In your business, you have many lines of different commerce. The easiest business you can start and most common one to all YOU.Incorporated owners is their labor business. In this business line, you exchange knowledge, skills, time, and physical labor for money. It's the simplest business you have. The money you get from this business line fuels most of the investments you are able to make in your other line of businesses.

The next type of business you likely have is an investment business. This business takes excess income from your labor business and invests it to create a passive stream of income in the future. A possible third line of business you have is a real estate business. This business is where you buy real estate actively through direct ownership or indirectly to produce further income streams in the future. A possible fourth line of business is what I call a "self-starter project" business. This line of business can be created from scratch or acquired by you. Such businesses are usually owned by you entirely or with partners. Those businesses are the most common lines you will find within You.Incorporated business owners but not the only ones.

All those lines of business produce an income stream that flows back into your YOU.Incorporated business. Since you are the sole owner and CEO of your YOU.Incorporated, you decide how best to allocate the incomes among your various business lines. For example, you might decide your labor business can see significant income increase if you invest in additional skill upgrades. Alternatively, you might decide to allocate more resources toward your real estate business as you see the return to be better than in other areas.

YOU. INCORPORATED

You are the business. Your job isn't your business.
YOU are the business and YOU are the CEO and SOLE OWNER.

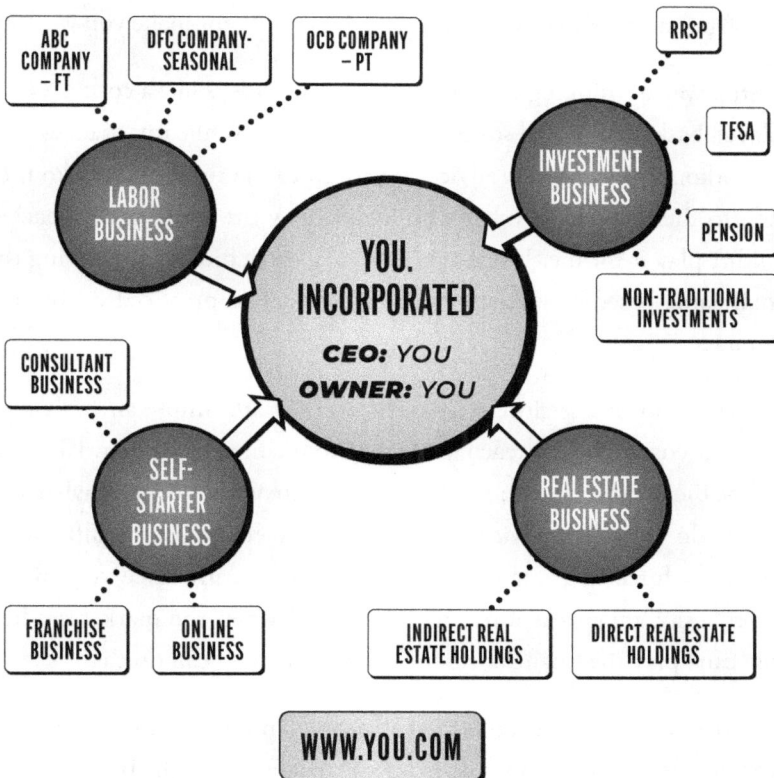

The YOU.Incorporated mindset works best because it matches up with the incentive structure of a capitalist system. If you're prepared to take ownership and risk, then your reward will be far greater than those who don't take ownership and adopt a dependency mindset.

Build your You.Incorporated business, and never let yourself believe you work for anyone. You only work for one company and that's You. Incorporated, of which you are the sole owner and CEO.

8. A financial advisor will not make you wealthy

There's a strange assumption in society that a good financial advisor is one who can make you wealthy. People don't say it outright, but that's the underlying reason they seek a financial advisor.

Let me be absolutely clear: A financial advisor will not make you wealthy.

A better way of thinking of a financial advisor's role is like a coach. When I played basketball, I had some amazing coaches. While my coaches gave me workouts and the best advice, it was up to me to do the workout or listen to their advice. It was I who had to play the game as my coaches couldn't play it for me. It was up to me to make adjustments during the actual game based on what my coaches and I had practiced during my workouts.

A financial advisor is similar to a coach. They are simply an individual trying to coach you to reach your maximum financial potential. They are not there to make you wealthy because they can't control what you actually do with their advice or force you to work on your wealth game. They can't force you not to spend money, they can't force you to put money away, they can't force you not to sell when the market crashes. They can't play the financial game for you, only you can do that.

Some people might seek a financial advisor as an insurance policy to have someone else to blame for their lack of ownership with their financial situation. Sometimes, we want to have someone to blame to avoid being accountable.

This section of the book is more or less my being your financial coach. I am sharing with you concepts and strategies that I believe can assist you on your financial journey. But I can't force you to adopt these strategies or accept these concepts. You are the one who actually has to do the work. You have to decide if you are willing to investigate these concepts, adopt them, and act on them in your life. That's up to you, and your success will not be a result of my sharing these concepts but rather when you put in the work.

That's all a financial advisor is—a coach. Now, just because you have a coach that doesn't mean you will be successful. Some coaches are better than others. Some players excel under one coach while they struggle under other. You need to believe and trust your coach. It's a relationship that's entirely based on trust. I trusted my basketball coaches because I knew they would provide honest advice, were extremely knowledgeable about the game, and they were excellent players when they played and had accomplished what I was trying to accomplish. But most importantly, each of my various coaches had an interest and purpose in my being successful.

It's important to find a financial advisor who can help you on your financial journey but understand that your financial advisor will not create wealth for you as only you can do that. If you are seeking a financial coach and would like to work with me directly, please visit www.wealthmarathon. com for more details.

9. Avoid the poverty mindset trap

That concept doesn't appear to be about wealth at first, but it is. It's also meant to help those of you who are struggling financially or feel like the system is stacked against you.

Say you're a single mother trying to raise a kid and doing everything that you are supposed to do, but you continue to struggle to even buy basic things for your kid. You rightfully get frustrated, to put it mildly. You feel as though you've been sold something that wasn't true. When you look around and you see other people doing well with their family, you get jealous, which turns to anger. Other people have multiple cars, houses, rental properties, travel, and so much more than just the basics. You see them going out for dinner with their kids, sending their kids to special camps, or enrolling them in special programs.

Now, you're not going to like what I have to say next, but you should keep reading. When you spend your entire energy and focus on being upset at what people have that you don't have, you condition your mind into believing that you can't do anything about your situation. That's the poverty mindset trap. It creates an accepted mindset that spending your energy pointing out the unfairness in life is the same thing as working toward making things better for yourselves. It's not.

You have to learn to stop falling for the poverty mindset. It encourages you to give up the most important tool you have to improving your situation, which is your mind. Instead of making jokes about the rich family and how out of touch they might be, go have dinner with them and learn how they earned their money. Instead of being mad at investors who make their money from real estate, find a way to learn how they built their business. Put your energy into learning how people obtained what you want and don't have, rather than using their success as an excuse to not try. The reason most successful people became successful is that they learned from other successful people.

If you grew up without money or struggled with money, you have an advantage. When you don't have money, you don't derive your value from money. I call those circumstances the gift and the curse. It's a gift because it means you don't need money to actually make yourself happy and you can become less emotional about it. But it's also a curse because it means you likely have money troubles and sometimes the pain is too much, which then brings you back to using all your energy to try and show how unjust your situation has been and currently is.

Yes, you have a gift, but you have to learn to move beyond the pain to utilize this gift. I wasn't poor, but my parents' experience early in Canada meant I saw how unfair the system can be for some. My family and I weren't wealthy by a lot of standards. We struggled financially upon arriving in Canada as my parents were becoming accustomed to Canada's financial system. The gift I got from my parents is I have never derived my value from money. I think I avoided the curse due to my parents' thirst and encouragement for learning, which I picked up. My desire to learn about money wasn't to derive my worth from it but rather to simply learn how the system worked. Therefore, money does not do anything for me regarding my value as a human being, which makes me really good at the impact of money.

Avoid being trapped by the poverty mindset and learn to understand the money system. You will make it fairer for all in the long run. It's your choice but be cautious of the poverty mindset as it always feels good but will never actually results in improvement of your situation.

10. Avoid the rich mindset trap

When we are born, we do not get to pick what family we are born into. Some of you are born into a family that is financially successful or wealthy. The rich mindset trap, for me, is avoiding the snares that such a financial upbringing can create.

If you're born into a so-called wealthy family, you should want to avoid rich mindset trap. The guilt created by this trap will create a set of behaviors in which you spend your energy trying to show people you are not rich instead of spending the energy toward equalizing the system.

Instead of actually working on the issue, you end up giving lip service to ensure people don't see you as too "upper class."

If you grew up with fewer financial challenges, it's important to recognize that situation isn't the norm for everyone. Since humans tend to hang with people who share similar backgrounds, you might believe it is the same for your group. You also might start to believe that people's lack of work ethic is the sole reason for their not being able to achieve financial success. That's the second trapping of a rich mindset. You're afraid of competition; therefore, you continue to support systems that are skewed toward your maintaining your advantage.

But you don't need to be afraid of competition. If you are a smart and capable person, it doesn't matter what family you are born into so long as you have equal opportunity. That's really your challenge. Learning to understand more fair and equal opportunity everyone has in the system will translate into a more stable system and life for you. Don't spend your energy trying to pretend as though you don't have financial advantages. You do, and everyone around you knows you do.

Lastly, be mindful that your challenge will be to change a system that will likely take away from the advantages you've had and increase greater competition for you. In the short run, the adjustment will reduce your wealth, but in the long run you will create a more balanced and sustainable system in which people compete based on their abilities and work ethic. What family you are born into will play less of a determination in your life or financial success.

11. Learn how to use credit effectively

Credit can become and feel like a drug. It starts off as an innocent curiosity or legitimate need that can lead to an addiction. Similar to drugs, credit has a strong psychological effect on the brain and your behavior when it comes to money. Often, before you come to realize you have a credit problem, you are so far in debt that the only option left is a cold hard detox known as bankruptcy.

People can become addicted to credit if their credit knowledge is low, which results in them overconsuming credit.

When everything is bought on credit, which is the most frequent method, it's easy to continue to consume without thinking twice about the long-term impact. Credit enables you to live the life you want today even if you can't afford it now or in the future. That's the effect credit has on the human mind and behavior. Its slogan reads the same as the much beloved shoemaker Adidas, "impossible is nothing." And nothing is impossible when you have access to credit.

But like any life built on a temporary high, it eventually comes crashing down. It's human nature to believe the good times will go on forever because credit provides the ultimate high, even though it comes at the risk of financial disaster.

It's important to have some basic understanding on how best to use credit. Here are two simple principles you need to be aware of when it comes to credit, which will assist in your effective usage of it.

The first thing is about credit leverage. Credit allows you to increase your income level today, while reducing your future income. For example, your salary is $40,000, and you get approved for a line of credit for $10,000. Your potential income level has increased to $50,000 today. While credit can enable you to increase your income today, it does so at the expense of your future income. Using the same example, if you were to utilize the full $10,000 line of credit, you've now committed your future income stream toward paying back the $10,000 plus any associated interest payment. Therefore, your future income has been reduced be $10,000 plus the associated interest. The number of years by which your future income stream is reduced depends on how long it takes you to pay back the debt.

The second thing you need to understand about credit is the concept of servicing. The term servicing simply means the ability for the debt acquired by credit to produce an income stream sufficient at a minimum to cover the debt payment obligations. Utilizing credit isn't a bad thing if you understand the importance of servicing the debt. Businesses use credit to help produce or acquire assets that produce an income stream sufficient enough to at least cover the credit cost. The concept also applies to individuals. When you use credit, you should use it to generate an income stream immediately or in the long run to service the debt payment. The perfect scenario is being able to service the debt payment plus generating additional income, but at minimum you should use credit only to obtain items that can generate an income stream sufficient to service the debt payment.

Real estate investing (not homeownership) is a perfect example of effective credit usage. An investor leverages their current income level to obtain enough credit to purchase a rental property. The property they purchase with their increased credit capacity produces an income in the form of rental payment that needs to capture the debt payment as well as a profit after all expenses are paid. Over time, similar to a business, the rental property increases the individual's income level while paying down the debt they borrowed and becomes an asset they can leverage. That's a great way to use credit.

12. Keep an eye on all your fees, particularly those that tend to be hidden

When I worked at the bank, I always was amazed at how many fees people paid and didn't even know they were paying. I would have clients who had multiple accounts they were paying for at different financial institutions, but only actively used one of those accounts. When I tried to persuade them to close the other accounts they weren't using, they would not take my advice and would continue paying for multiple accounts they didn't use.

Fees matter a great deal if you're working toward financial independence. Every penny you give to someone else is money that you can't pay yourself with. Therefore, you need to check everything you pay for and ask yourself if the fee you are paying is really worth the service or product you get.

Check all your fees to ensure they make sense. Most people never shop around for accounts such as their cell phone, cable, home insurance, or internet service to name a few. We tend to just accept whatever fees we are being charged and never bother to review them to see if perhaps we can lower them. It's why many people are still paying banks a fee to hold their money.

There are countless fee-free banking options that are owned by the big banks, which will charge nothing to store your physical or digital money. Who needs to be paying a bank $10 per month to give you money that the bank will leverage to make more money for itself?

Every penny you pay in fees is money you lose.

13. Avoid bad debts

Is debt good or bad? It can be an emotional topic, especially the emotional toll debt can take on a person, which I've seen firsthand. In my journey to learn more about money, I've developed a more holistic understanding of debt.

I think of debt like the fat around our body. I know, I know, but stay with me a little longer. We all know our body requires some fat (at least if you want to be healthy), and you can't avoid having fat. We also know that in certain places on our body, fat is actually a positive thing. The trick with body fat and debt is to ensure you have the right amount in the right places and not so much that it becomes detrimental to your lifestyle and health. There you have it—debt is like body fat.

Therefore, believing that debt is always bad is an incomplete understanding of the concept. The truth is there are good debts and bad debts, and you want to strive to have only good debts. The simplest way to determine if you have good or bad debt is by answering two simple questions. First, is there a cash flow stream associated with the debt? If so, who is paying the cash flow or receiving the cash flow stream?

For example, credit card debt that doesn't produce income for you is bad debt because it doesn't increase your cash flow. A credit card company doesn't normally pay you money for the balances you owe them. The same is true for a mortgage on a principal residence.

What's interesting about debt is most people do not focus on the cash flow stream attached to their associated debt obligations. Someone will buy a home and consider it a good debt because they believe it will be worth more in the future, but they fail to understand for the next 25+ years that debt doesn't produce any cash flow stream. Car loans are another example of bad debt. A car might enable you to get a better job, which might improve your overall cash flow, but the specific debt associated with the car loan takes away cash flow in order to service the debt, and the asset (car) depreciates over time, which reduces its value over time.

The trick with debt is to understand how to leverage it to produce additional cash flow for you.

Cash flow is so important because it's what you live on. We require a certain amount of money each month to maintain our lifestyle. When you can increase your cash flow, you are able to allocate it (or some of it) to the lifestyle you want.

Using the cash flow definition will quickly tell you if you've acquired good debt or bad debt. However, be mindful that just because you have good debt now that doesn't mean it can't become bad debt.

When taking on good debt, do it at a manageable pace. Don't overextend yourself even if the debt produces a good cash flow. Keep your bad debt load as low as possible while maximizing on the possible cash flow stream. Note, I said low, not zero, because it's almost impossible for you not to carry some form of bad debt temporarily at some point in your life. If we all had zero debt, our economy would come to a grinding halt. When you decide to take on debt, do it on things that appreciate in value over time and more importantly also produce an income stream.

14. Understand and utilize compound interest

There are certain things you learn in life that change how you see things. For me, it was understanding the difference between simple interest and compound interest. Most of us have a general understanding of the difference between the two, but few of us truly appreciate why these two concepts are important to understand early in life.

Let's tackle the easy one, simple interest. In short, simple interest calculates interest based on the original principal balance. For example, let's assume you deposited $500 into a savings account paying 4% interest annually. After year one, you would have $520, which is a combination of the original principal of $500 and $20 of interest earned. In the second year, you would have a total value of $540, which again is a combination of your original $500 plus $20 of interest earned from year one and an additional $20 in new interest earned for year two.

With simple interest, the interest paid is always calculated based on the original principal that was deposited. In year two, the opening balance was $520 but the interest payment was still being calculated on the opening balance, which was $500.

Compound interest on the other hand, calculates interest on the initial balance as well as any interest that might have been earned on top of the principal. To calculate it, you need to know the compounding period in addition to principal, interest rate, and the number of years you will be investing/saving. Depending on the product, the compounding period could be monthly, daily, quarterly, weekly, semi-annually, or annually. Using our original example, let's keep the same initial deposit of $500 with an annual interest rate of 4%, compounded annually over two years. By the end of year two, you will have accumulated a total balance of $540.80.

That's the power of compounding. You just made an extra $0.80 by doing nothing! You might be thinking, what's the big deal? It's only $0.80 more than simple interest. But here's big difference: Compounding cycles can go on indefinitely, which means you can continue to earn interest on interest forever.

If the compounding period and rate remained the same on the initial deposit but over a 20-year period, you would have accumulated a total interest of $595.56 compared to only $400 with simple interest on the starting balance of $500. You just made an extra $195.56 in interest for doing nothing! Things get even more interesting when you deposit a larger starting balance.

Let's assume you had $50,000 deposited and held it for 10 years with an interest rate of 4% compounded annually. By the end of the 10 years, your total balance will be $74,012.21, with $24,012.21 of that amount being interest you earned on your original $50,000 deposit. The same example, using simple interest would amount to a total balance of $70,000, with only $20,000 of that balance being interest earned on the initial deposit. The additional $4,012.21 earned was a result of the power of compounding, which gives you interest on interest. When it comes to compounding, the earlier you start, the more your money will do more of the work for you.

While I illustrated the power of compounding using an investment example, it's important to also realize the power of compounding works the same on debts. Compounding works the same way when you borrow money and don't pay off your credit card balance in full. Someone gets a big Grinch-like smile on their face, simply because you failed to understand the power of compounding interest.

To illustrate the importance of time and compound interest, here's a popular story that's often told to clients who want to invest.

Two sisters—let's call them Seville and Valencia—each invested in the market to save toward retirement. While both sisters invested in the market, each went about it differently.

Seville started investing right after high school. She was putting away as much as she could with her part-time job—say $500 per month. She would continue her monthly savings throughout college and after landing her first career job. But after 25 years of putting away $500 per month, she ran into some financial difficulties due to some medical issues. As a result, Seville wasn't able to work as much and needed her investment money now to cover her daily medical cost, which meant she had to stop contributing the $500 per month she had been investing for her retirement after 25 years of doing so each month.

Valencia also invested in the market, but she didn't make the same investment decisions as Seville, at least not right away. Valencia got a job after high school and continued to work while in college. After she graduated, she also was able to land a nice career job. During her time after high school and upon landing her career job, she was earning enough to be able to save $500 toward her retirement but she didn't invest her money like her sister Seville.

She was more interested in travelling and doing other interesting things at the time with her extra savings. So, her extra $500 mostly went into her travel adventures and hobbies. Investing wasn't really something she worked on or thought about until 25 years later. After seeing her sister go through her health issues, she started to realize she didn't have anything put away if she experienced the same thing as her sister did and wasn't able to work.

Fearing what would happen to her if she had health problems, she decides to start investing to build her retirement savings. Since she was late to the game, she asked her sister how much she had put toward building her retirement savings. Seville advised her that she previously was putting away $500 per month. After getting this information, Valencia decided since she was late to investing, she would double what her sister had put away in an effort to build her retirement savings quickly. Valencia committed to putting away $1,000 per month for the next 25 years. As such, she started investing 25 years after her sister ended her monthly investment contribution as a result of her health issues.

Now, which sister do you think ends up with more money? If you said Seville, you would be correct. That common investment story is meant to illustrate two primary concepts: time and power of compounding. It's always better to invest whatever you can as soon as you can than to wait before you start investing. Money requires time to grow, and compounding interest just keeps rolling once it gets going.

Here are the final numbers based on the assumption that the rate of return for each sister was 5%, compounded annually over the 25 years.

Seville after 25 years of investing has a total investment portfolio balance is $292,867.26. Her total interest earned up to that point works out to be $142,867.26 while her principal contribution works out to be $150,000.

Valencia at the end of her investing period of 25 years has a total portfolio balance of $585,734.52, not bad, right? Her principal contribution is $300,000 while the interest earned is $285,734.52.

But didn't I say Seville had more money? She does. See, Valencia started later in life after her sister Seville's investment had already been growing for 25 years.

As a result of her early investing, Seville already had a balance $292,867.26 before she was unable to invest any new contribution, which is when Valencia started saving toward her invest for her retirement. As such, Seville has a 25-year head start over her sister. Valencia realizes it, and that's why she decides to double her investment contribution in an effort to make up for lost time. However, she's unable to reduce the gap due to the power of compounding and time.

As a result of Seville's head start, her total investment period is actually 50 years not 25 years. Remember, she started 25 years before her sister; therefore, the total time her money has to grow is 50 years. As a result of this long investment period, Seville's total investment value is $991,751.61, which is based on the $292,867 balance after 25 years, earning 5% annually and compounded annually for another 25 years.

Compounding is a beautiful thing really.

That often-told investment story always puts a smile on my face. Invest whatever you can today because money requires time to grow. When time and the power of compounding join forces, the amount of money you can earn is only limited by how soon you start to plant your money seeds. Invest today no matter how small of an amount you have in order to utilize the power of compounding and time.

15. Why most people fail at investing in the stock market

My first investment was in high school. My high school offered an elective course in finance that allowed me to trade stocks in a simulated game online. It was my first time trading stocks, and the simulation was meant to provide us with some real-life experience into how the stock market operated without losing real money. The course ran the entire semester, and it was one of the courses that really pushed me into finance. At the time, Google was trading around $300 per share. I felt it was too pricey at the time, which shows no one knows the future and was a sign of my stock-picking abilities.

Once I began university, I started investing with my own money after my first year. Despite my high school experience, I really had no clue what I was doing. My high school experience showed me it was possible to make money from the stock market, but I still had an educational and experience gap.

I would eventually invest my first $500 in a mutual fund after my first year of university. I had no clue what I was doing really, but thankfully the bank employee set me up on the right path. She invested my $500 into a balance mutual fund and insisted I set up an on-going pre-authorized contribution each month after my initial purchase. And that was it. She said don't do anything else and just keep contributing each month. Though I had traded stocks in a simulated environment, doing it with my own money was scary. But eventually I learned how it worked.

Investing can seem overwhelming as the options have increased dramatically today, and there's a choice overload. But it's simpler than it seems.

There are many factors that go into having a successful investment portfolio. Half of those factors can include things such as diversification, cost awareness, and time in the market.

But my advisor and personal experience revealed that most investors fail not only as a result of only those factors. Investor failures can also be linked back to their human behaviors. Many people will sell their investments the minute it goes down despite their advisor reminding them of their long-term objectives. Some investors tend to be overconfident about their investment abilities. They believe they can become a professional portfolio manager while raising a family and working full-time without taking any educational or certification courses on investment. Some investors believe speculating is the same thing as investing. They lack patience and are always looking to get rich quickly. They fail to understand investing is a marathon, not a sprint.

Others can feel intimidated, which can result in their failing to ask questions about their investments. They want complex solutions because they assume if it's complicated, it must be worth the cost. In believing so, they brush off simple solutions because it doesn't make them feel special, and they forget the stock market doesn't care about your feelings or situations you are going through. They blame the market, the advisor, their friend's advice, but will never look at their own investment behavior and actions that could have contributed to the poor performance of their investment.

Financial success is less about arithmetic and more about emotional discipline. The key to your success with money is to keep your emotions out of it, along with developing the right set of habits for financial success. To be successful at investing, you require emotional disciple and holding yourself accountable.

Most people are good at the initial phase of investing. They go to their local bank, speak to their advisor, determine their goals and objectives, purchase a basket of stocks with good diversification. But the true test comes when they leave their advisor's office and the market goes down.

That's where you see who truly understands investing and those who just like looking at numbers on their screen to be able to show to their friends.

Your advisor can provide you the best investment advice and strategy to follow to reach your goals, but all that is pointless if you do not follow through on the plan and strategy. A plan without action is just useless information.

It's important to hold yourself to a higher standard of accountability when it comes to your investments. Do the right things that are required for success and learn to keep it simple while having a long-term view. At minimum, avoid making poor investment decisions in the name of having interesting stock stories to discuss with your friends and family. This is your money, and accountability should start with and end with you.

16. Understand the approaches used to invest in the stock market

There are two primary methods you can use to invest in the market, active or passive. Each approach has its advantages and disadvantages. Therefore, it's important to understand the two methods in order to determine which method will work best for you. The goal here is to increase your knowledge level around investing in the stock market to enable you to better understand what's going on within your own investment account. That knowledge will enable you to have a more in-depth conversation with individuals who are assisting you with your investment. Let's start by understanding what passive investing is.

PASSIVE INVESTING OVERVIEW

Passive investing aims to replicate the return of a specific benchmark index such as the Standard & Poor's 500 (S&P 500) or Toronto Stock Exchange (TSX). The most common way to invest passively is through an index mutual fund or an exchange-traded fund (EFT).

The Toronto Stock Exchange is Canada's main stock market exchange and is where shares of all the publicly traded companies in Canada can be bought and sold. The returns of all these companies can be tracked individually or as a collective. An index tracks the total return of all the companies that make up the specific index. There are many indices around the world. For example, the U.S. has the S&P 500 index and Nasdaq index. The key takeaway is that when you hear of an index return, they are referring to the collective return of all companies within that index.

If someone is using a passive investment approach as their method of investing, they are trying to replicate the collective return of a specific index, which they are tracking as closely as possible before fees. In Canada, they would be trying to replicate the total return of all the companies that make up the Toronto Stock Exchange.

The way an investor achieves the collective return of the benchmark index is fairly straightforward, at least in theory. The investor would buy the stock of every single company that makes up the Toronto Stock Exchange. In doing so, they hope to then replicate the collective return of the exchange before fees. The investor would sell and buy based on companies being removed or added to the benchmark index, not based on what he or she believed was the best company with the best outlook necessarily.

Today, an investor doesn't have to buy shares in each individual company listed on the exchange to replicate the return of an index. Instead, you simply buy an index mutual fund or an exchange traded fund (ETF) for the specific index you wish to track.

Someone who uses a passive investment strategy isn't trying to outperform the index. Rather, they want to replicate the index return minus any fees they might incur to replicate that return.

WHY PICK A PASSIVE INVESTMENT STRATEGY?

An investor who picks a passive investment strategy over an active one believes the market is efficient. They believe the market has already factored in all the relevant information available about a company or the market. Therefore, there isn't any real advantage in spending additional resources trying to get an edge over the market in that the price reflects all the relevant information available. Passive investors believe over the long term it's hard for an active strategy to outperform the market.

Passive investing is also attractive to investors who are looking for more of a hands-off approach to their investment. Passive investing requires less daily research since you're simply taking the market return for whatever index you're tracking. But perhaps the biggest reason people opt for passive investing is due to fees. Passive investing offers much lower fees than an actively managed mutual fund due to its simply replicating a return. Over an investor's lifetime, those fees can have a significant impact on the amount of return an investor takes home.

A passive strategy can be used for both equity (stocks) and debt securities (bonds).

Advantages of passive investing:
- Lower fees compared to an active strategy
- Fairly simple to start
- Success based less on the investor's abilities
- Lower chance of underperforming the market
- Lower trading fees
- Less portfolio turnover
- More tax efficient

Disadvantages of passive investing:

- ➔ Returns of the benchmark or index below your investment goal or objective
- ➔ Can underperform an active strategy
- ➔ No guarantee the returns will match the benchmark or index return exactly
- ➔ Lacks excitement (less frequent trading, less stock talk at parties)
- ➔ Less direct control over specific investment holdings
- ➔ Harder to take advantage of market opportunities

The important thing to remember about the passive investment strategy is you're buying everything in the belief that over the long-term the market(s) operates efficiently and eliminates your biggest barrier of cost and you. Therefore, a passive strategy keeps the cost low, while moving you out of the way of your own success by letting the market do its thing.

ACTIVE INVESTING OVERVIEW

An active investment strategy focuses on selecting or creating a portfolio of investments that will beat the performance of an equivalent benchmark or market index return.

Active strategies fall into two categories: top-down or bottom-up approach. A top-down approach starts by looking at the overall economy for opportunities while a bottom-up approach focuses on a particular stock or sector for opportunities. An active strategy can be used for both equity and debt securities.

WHY PICK AN ACTIVE INVESTMENT STRATEGY?

An investor who uses an active investment strategy believes that markets are not efficient on their own. They believe the price of an asset doesn't always reflect all information available; therefore, there are opportunities to generate greater returns by investing resources to know and obtain that additional information. An active investor doesn't simply buy all the stocks trading on a stock market, rather they buy the best group of stocks they believe will likely generate a greater return than if he or she had simply bought the entire index.

Another less admitted reason for picking this strategy is it fulfills our need to be right and, on some level, our competitive nature as humans. I'm not saying everyone using an active strategy is looking to be right, but an active strategy is a "sport," and most investors do not even have the right gear to participate.

Advantages of active investing:

- Possible to beat the benchmark index
- Direct control over investment being selected
- More investment strategies to select from

Disadvantages associated with active investing:

- Tax inefficient
- Investment return based entirely on the skills and ability of the investor
- Difficult to beat the market consistently over a long period
- Higher fees compared to passive investing

An investor who uses an active strategy may generate a greater return relative to the benchmark index against which it's being compared. The investor achieves that goal through an in-depth analysis to try and find an edge about a stock or sector. The most common way to access an active strategy is through mutual funds or by investing on your own through a brokerage account. Fees associated with an active strategy are generally higher than with a passive strategy. However, higher fees might be justified if the returns are high enough to offset the cost while still beating the benchmark or achieving your desired rate of return after fees.

If you believe you can beat the market or would like to beat the market, an active strategy is the way to go. But be warned: Beating the market is easier said than done, especially consistently.

WHICH STRATEGY SHOULD YOU PICK FOR YOUR INVESTMENT?

There's no shortage of financial analysis, blogs, or television commentary about passive versus active investment strategy. But here's bottom line: Over a long investment cycle, a passive investment strategy is likely to outperform an active strategy, all things being equal. And if you think about it, that likelihood makes sense.

Let's use the sprint Olympics event to explain what I mean. Usain Bolt had won Olympic gold medals in each of the following sprint events: 100 meters, 200 meters. His winnings came at the Rio 2016, London 2012, and Beijing 2008 Olympics.[82] He also won gold in the 4×100-meter relay in the London 2012 and Rio 2016 Olympics.[83] That's a total of eight gold medals over nine years. For nine years he was the greatest Olympic sprinter in the events in which he won gold. But even as great as Usain Bolt was during those nine years, even he knew he couldn't sustain that type of performance indefinitely or even for another nine years.

Active investors also can be right for nine years, but as the investment time increases, it becomes increasingly more difficult for them to continue to be right. The keyword is not impossible but just more difficult as time goes on since no one knows the future.

---

82 "Usain Bolt," Olympics, accessed August 13, 2021, https://olympics.com/en/athletes/usain-bolt.

83 Ibid.

In a weird way, Usain Bolt is an active investment strategy. If any great active investment managers would have selected Usain Bolt over the last nine years, they would have made their investors a lot of money. A passive investment manager would have bought a little piece of each sprinter over that same nine-year period, including Usain Bolt. Their return would have been good, but nothing like the return of the investors who only bought investment in Usain Bolt.

When people say active investing is better than passive investing, it can be misleading. If there were a clear winner, then any debate would not continue. I believe both need each other in order to play to their audience. Passive investors need active managers who try and beat the market but over the long term come up short. An active strategy needs investors who want to try and beat the market, even if it might only be for a short period.

Either strategy could work when done right. What's important is to understand what you're buying, as well as the strategy you've picked to help you reach your investment objectives based on your risk profile.

IT'S LESS ABOUT THE PASSIVE OR ACTIVE APPROACH AND MORE ABOUT FEES

When it comes to the long-term return performance between active versus passive, the data points to a clear winner. In an article written for Index Fund Advisor, based on information collected from the 2020 SPIVA U.S. Scorecard, 86% of all domestic U.S. funds underperformed their respective benchmark.[84] The period being tracked was from January 1, 2001 to December 31, 2020. During the same period, 86.55% of global funds underperformed their respective benchmarks, while 97.96% of Fixed Income Government Long Funds underperformed

---

84 Murray Coleman, "SPIVA: 2020 Full-Year Active vs. Passive Scorecard," Index Fund Advisors, updated March 29, 2021, https://www.ifa.com/articles/despite_brief_reprieve_2018_spiva_report_reveals_active_funds_fail_dent_indexing_lead_-_works/.

their benchmark.[85] The longer the time period, the harder it becomes for an active fund to continue to outperform its benchmark consistently. However, I believe that it's still possible to use an active strategy for your entire portfolio or a portion of it. I also believe that you can use a passive investment strategy for your entire portfolio or for some of it. The choice is less about active or passive and more about fees, fees, and fees.

Fees can eat away at investment returns like termites eat through wood. Investment fees follow the same idea as compound interest, but it's money coming out of your portfolio.

THE IMPACT OF FEES ON INVESTMENT RETURNS

Let's assume you have two investments. Both investments have an annual contribution of $1,200. The annual rate of return for both investments is 5%. The only difference between the two investments is their fee structure, commonly known as management expense ratio (MER). Investment A has an MER of 2% while investment B has an MER of 0.80%.

After 25 years of investing, both investments will be worth $60,136. The associated fee for Investment A works out to $15,072, which results in a total investment value of $45,064. The associated fee with Investment B works out to be $6,637 for a total investment value of $53,499. I will say it again, all things being equal, fees obviously matter a great deal.

PICK WHAT WILL ENABLE YOU TO BE SUCCESSFUL

I think for the average person who is raising a family, working, and just trying to live but has no interest in really managing their own investment, a passive strategy is the best way to go or an actively managed fund with low management fees. If you do go the active approach route, however, keep in mind over the long term it's hard to consistently beat the market. If you are compelled to take the active route, an actively managed fund

85   Ibid.

with low fees with good diversification is a must. Aim for a fund that carries no more than 1.5% MER fee, if possible, while ensuring their performance isn't below the benchmark consistently.

People make money using an active strategy, and people make money using a passive strategy—that's why both are still around. Regardless of your strategy, fees are really what will kill your investment return if you do not keep an eye on it. That's not to say you should simply go with the cheapest product. Rather, if you have two highly regarded funds that are equal in every way but the fee, you should pick the one with the lower fee. Keep your fees low, ensure you are well diversified, contribute consistently, re-balance at least once per year, and keep the focus on the long term. If you can do that, you are likely to be successful with your investment over the long term.

17. Protect your human capital

The most important asset is not your job or your house, it's you. I can't stress enough how important it is to protect yourself. Protecting your human capital doesn't only mean things like eating right or going to the gym every day but should also include mental well-being.

Learn to love who you are. That means if you're going through a difficult time in your life, you need to reach out to trusted family and friends. Mental illness or challenges don't need to be suffered in isolation. Some of the toughest battles we face in life are in our heads. Most of the mental challenges we face stem from our building our love foundation based on other people's love. If your love foundation isn't built first with you as the foundation, then the minute you have an issue in life, face difficulty or criticism, your foundation will crumble.

A house that sits on solidly built foundation can be rebuilt even if it is destroyed.

And lastly, do the essential things to protect your income and those who depend on you financially. Don't buy a home if you don't have a life insurance policy in place or home insurance. Look into disability insurance because chances are you will get hurt at some point. You are the most important asset, and you need to protect your human capital because without you there is no wealth creation, or worse, no income for those who depend on you.

18. Don't base your lifestyle on other people's end results

The type of lifestyle you live has a large impact on your financial well-being. Many of us are guilty of falling in love with other people's success. The problem with falling in love with someone's life is it often doesn't tell you the full story or provide any insight into the process that created what you desire. We tend to model our lifestyle based on other people's instead of finding out how they achieved the lifestyle we envy.

When we see someone like Jay-Z, many of us want his lifestyle even if our income doesn't support such a lifestyle. Being inspired by Jay-Z to want a better life for yourself is a good thing, but trying to have his lifestyle even when your ability and skills don't support such a lifestyle can cause financial and emotional stress.

To live a lifestyle that's reflective of your abilities and skills requires you to be comfortable with the lifestyle that your skills and abilities are able to provide to you. Therefore, the goal isn't to compete with other people's lifestyle, but rather have a lifestyle that's based on your skills and abilities.

If a friend has a certain lifestyle that you find desirable, the first thing is to determine if both your skills and abilities are similar to theirs. If that's true, then they might be a good model to follow. Next, you want to find out more about the individual's context or process that led to their lifestyle. How they achieved it will tell you the level of work as well as the skills and abilities required to have such a lifestyle. An unexamined view of another's life is similar to only seeing the end of a movie. Yes, you know how the movie ended, but you don't know how that ending came about. Finding out how another achieved what they have requires seeing the context of the whole movie.

19. Time is the most valuable commodity you have

How long do you think you will live for? Let me ask the question a different way. How long do you hope to live for? I want you to give the answer some thought, so pause here to come up with a number. Got the number? Okay.

Now, how much control do you have to reach that age? We have some, but we certainly don't have total control. You could avoid every bad thing that's been known to bring death or speed it up in humans and still end up not reaching your number.

This dynamic is what makes time the most precious and only truly valuable commodity we each have. We can overvalue our time or undervalue it. I bet you never thought of your time and life expectancy as a supply and demand thing.

Therefore, how you spend or what you do with your money should be based around the understanding that time is the only truly valuable commodity. It's why I believe getting a mortgage that provides you with more financial options is wiser than buying a home that might be a good investment but requires a mortgage that reduces your financial options when all you can do is meet your mortgage payment. You will have a far more enriched life experience if you work toward creating financial freedom for yourself sooner than later.

20. Globalization shouldn't be feared. It should be embraced

Who says you have to live and retire in the same country you were born in? Globalization has made retirement and wealth creation easier, in my opinion. Who says outsourcing is only for businesses or the ultra-wealthy? Learn to plan and look at things from a global standpoint.

If you only focus on what's in your backyard, you might be missing out on some huge opportunities. The reality is we are moving into a borderless world with the help of technology, and while some continue to fight that change, my advice to you is stop fighting and look for the potential opportunities it offers to you and those you care for.

I know of some people who think globalization is a bad thing. Part of the problem we have as humans is we tend to think in the short term. Globalization worked well for some countries initially as they had a clear competitive knowledge advantage. Today, most countries have adopted some form of capitalism, which naturally makes it more competitive. Now, some countries that benefited tremendously in the initial stages of capitalism are finding they are not benefiting as much. But the reality isn't that these countries aren't benefiting as much; rather the truth is more of the pie isn't going to them anymore because other countries have invested and have reduced the knowledge gap around globalism. Regardless, there's is no going away from globalization at this point, but it will have to evolve like anything else in life. The realities that you need to be aware of are that everyone more or less now has access to the same knowledge and to be glad that direction has made us more equal even though it will be painful as we move to the new, more balance dynamic.

Companies have mostly benefited from globalization due to access to cheaper labor and a bigger talent pool.[86] If you want to start a clothing company today, you would seek out production in a country that has the cheapest labor possible, unless you can justify a high price tag and a sense of country pride to employ more expensive workers. The same advantage is now also possible for individuals. You can take advantage of lower cost

---

86 Theodore Levitt, "The Globalization of Markets," *Harvard Business Review*, May 1983, https://hbr.org/1983/05/the-globalization-of-markets.

of living in other parts of the world and bring your talent and knowledge to assist those places in their desire to have more of the economic pie.

Today, many people are moving to and residing in other parts of the world that have lower cost of living, while still earning their income in their native country where the currency is stronger.[87] For example, you could be a Canadian citizen and work or have a business operating in Canada, yet you reside in Bali full-time. You have high income being paid in Canadian dollars, but your cost of living is much lower in Bali. Your income goes further there because in Canada a large percentage of your income would be tied to putting a roof over your head, which would leave you with less disposable income. Such an approach even has a name: the Nomadic Life.[88]

I'm not suggesting you move to Bali but rather trying to point out the opportunities available to you and also the importance that expenses play in the quality of life you can have, which is another reason to keep your mortgage debt low. If you're able to keep your fixed cost low while keeping a high-income level, you're likely to have a decent quality of life compared to someone earning a high income but high expenses.

Globalization, like anything in life, isn't perfect. There are problems with it, but I also want you to be mindful there are benefits too. Rather than being fearful of globalization, be open to the opportunities and benefits it can offer to you and your family.

21. Be mindful of who's in your inner circle

My family and I moved around a lot when I was a kid. After the first few moves, I was done with the word "moving." The biggest thing I hated

---

87 "Want to Work Remotely Abroad? Try These 12 Cities for Digital Nomads," Thrillist, updated February 3, 2021, https://www.thrillist.com/travel/nation/best-cities-in-the-world-working-remotely-cheap.

88 Ibid.

about moving as a kid was having to make new friends. Making friends as a kid is tough enough on its own but being the only black kid every couple of years at new school made it more challenging. Thankfully, my saving grace to this problem as I got older was that I was a little athletic. Turns out everyone wants to be friends with the athlete no matter how new you are.

I recall every time we had to move my dad always tried to play down the move and focus on all the great things the new place will bring us. But one day he said something that has stayed with me my entire life. He said, "You will lose friends and gain new friends throughout your life." Sounds like a simple advice, but that's a pretty honest and powerful statement to tell a young kid.

As an adult, I've come to appreciate friends, but more importantly I've learned the importance of having the right kind of friends around me. Many of us have friends, but most of us don't have the right kind or type of friends. What do friends and creating wealth have to do with each other? A lot! Next to your family, friends have the biggest influence on your financial habits and decisions.

As such, it's important to know the type of friends who are likely to create bad financial habits that will prevent you from reaching financial independence. Please note, I am not speaking of the character of people but rather the behavior or habits certain friends display that can be bad for your finances.

There are two particular types of friends I want you to be aware of. The first group is the social spender. This group of friends always seems to cost you money whenever you hang out with them. Take a moment and think about any friend or group of friends who might fit that group. Reduce the amount of time you spend with this person or group of people as you will constantly be spending money to feel good or to have a good time.

The second group of friends you want to be aware of is those who accept life as is and just want to get by. Here's a question for you. Does the script make the actor, or does the actor make the script? I don't know the answer, but this group definitely wants to be actors in a well-written script. Life doesn't always give us a nice script to work with, and ultimately how the final script turns out is based on your effort. Just accepting life's script shouldn't be an option.

Friends who match the second group impact your financial well-being more than the social spenders because the second group lacks ambition and just want to go with the flow of life, which hurts your biggest asset: your mind. If you live in North America or a country where the free market is the foundation of the economic system, hanging around someone who just wants to get by will hurt your financial drive. There's nothing wrong with just being like everyone else, but I'm assuming that's not your goal by still reading this.

Pay attention to those you surround yourself with. Hang around people who don't constantly take money away from your pocket or those who are unmotivated. Find people who are being successful in their field of interest or living the lifestyle you would like. Look for friends who inspire you, and avoid people who constantly make up reasons why life sucks. And yes, life does suck at times, but what's important is how you approach life's difficulties.

Be selective and be conscious of those in your inner circle as they will influence your financial habits more than you expect or would like to admit.

Please note once again, I am not saying someone's financial wealth or poor financial habits are a reflection of their worth. I am simply pointing out that the individuals you surround yourself with influence how you think and behave toward money.

22. Be skeptical of group consensus when it comes to wealth creation

Most group consensus is wrong because individuals stop thinking when placed within a group setting. I tend to be extremely skeptical of group thinking. If 9 of my 10 friends all share the same opinion, I know it's likely that the first person did the research, and the others just accepted the first person's conclusion. The 10th person just wants to be different, and likely didn't look into the issue either but didn't want to have the same position as the group.

That's generally how I approach groups, and I apply that concept until I find the truth for myself, which means I tend to move in the opposite direction. Social media is perhaps the best example of how the group consensus doesn't always work. How many of us start judging someone based on a headline or picture? We've all been guilty of it, including me. If it looks and fits with the headline, we re-tweet it or otherwise react to it before we we've even read the full content.

Individuals acting within a group make decisions that are more likely to be accepted by the group rather than making the right decision(s) based on the facts of the situation. Once you're placed within a group, you want the group's protection, and to get it you must act in the best interest of the group, even if those positions or decisions do not sit well with you personally. The group has a strong leverage on how we behave.

But group consensus isn't all bad. It can be used for positive things, such as encouraging us to treat each other better. The important thing is to think for yourself first and not simply go with the group consensus.

If you come to the same conclusion of the group based on your own review of the facts or situation, that's okay. You thought for yourself first, and your conclusion just happens to be what others thought as well. Sometimes, the smart thing in life is to not be forced to have an opinion on everything. There's no rule that says you can't simply say, "I do not have enough information on this matter; therefore, I cannot provide an opinion as it would not be helpful to the situation."

The group-think concept plays out with money a lot. People follow what their friends are doing with their money rather than first investigating things for themselves. As a result, you're more likely to want to buy when your friends are buying and sell when your friends are selling. If you want to be financially independent, you will have to at times make decisions that might go against group consensus when it comes to money or put you at odds within your group of friends and family.

That's why it's important to review the facts for yourself and then come to your own conclusion when making money decisions. Learn to think for yourself first. Understand, to think for yourself first will at times mean you risk the protection of the group. Still, think for yourself first to ensure you make the best decision for yourself and the situation you find yourself dealing with.

23. Establish relationships with people who are at least 20 years older than you

One of the secrets that's helped me better understand money is having friends who are much wiser than I am. My friends are smart, knowledgeable, and wonderful human beings. They have a lot of experience, and if you're smart, you'll listen to their stories and learn from them. When you're young, you tend to use the trial-and-error approach. That's how we learn. It's much better to learn from other people's mistake and avoid making the same mistakes if you can.

When you hang with people who are much older than you, they share their experiences and are able to provide honest feedback on experiences that you might be embarking on. If you listen and ask the right set of questions you can avoid making unnecessary mistakes. Having such valuable friends will not only make your life better but will also indirectly help your finances. By finding people who have reached a stage in their life where they are ready to give back in the form of sharing their successes— and most importantly, their failures—the next generation is able to learn what worked for them and what didn't.

Again, similar to my advice on the inner circle guide, I don't mean you should just go out and find people who are 20 years older than you and befriend them. That's not what I'm saying here, but if you happen to meet someone who is credible and you enjoy each other's company that results in a true friendship, you should cherish this relationship. You should pay attention to their stories and advice carefully. Probe them on their life journey to understand what they feel they did right or wrong and what they would do differently today. Then, you can evaluate the variables that might have resulted in their being successful or unsuccessful (they will tell you) and see if those variables apply to you and your current situation. Why learn from trial and error when you can just learn from other people's wisdom?

24. Be a shareholder, not only an employee

One of the ways I've been able to secure my employment throughout my career is having a shareholder mindset in every company I've worked at. When I first started my career, I was often just interested in just doing the work and wouldn't pay attention to actually how the company was doing. I soon realized, if I didn't understand how my company who paid me made money then I wouldn't know when the business wasn't doing well.

This mindset of seeing myself as a shareholder in addition to being a employee is the reason I left the financial advising role. When I became aware that I was the fourth advisor at my last advisor role, I realized the business model was no longer working. While the bank marketed itself to the public as being an advice-driven business, the reality was I wasn't able to do that as the business model was first driven by selling product(s).

My yearly target constantly meant that I had to make a choice between providing for my family or doing right by my client at the expense of my family. I thought this couldn't last. Furthermore, as the targets got higher the traffic to branches got lower. I started to hear clients being frustrated by our bank hours of 8 a.m. to 4 p.m., and they wanted and needed to have access accordingly to their availability as they also worked during those hours. I noticed younger people such as myself didn't really go to the bank, and I noticed blogging advice was becoming an increasing source of how younger people were getting their financial advice. They were no longer going to their parents' advisor because their parents' advisor wasn't discussing the challenges their generation was facing such as trying to buy a home that was becoming impossible to save up for.

When I put everything together, I could see that the pressure to produce results was increasing on me, but the business model would have to change as people were no longer banking as they used to. I realized I would constantly be stressed trying to produce in an environment that was no longer set up for the type of advising I was hired to do. People were changing their banking habits, but the bank was still expecting me to produce revenue as though people hadn't changed their banking habits.

If you work for a company, you have to understand you have legal insider information. As an employee, you have direct access to information and details that others do not. You are able to see if the company is doing well, you see if revenue is going up or down, you see if clients' habits are changing and if your company is adapting to those changes. When you see yourself as a shareholder and an employee, you have a vested interest in the company doing well. You want to know more about how your company works and if they have a good business model in place. Since you see yourself as a shareholder and not just an employee, you also don't buy into the feel-good story the CEO might tell you, but instead you analyze the business to see if what the CEO is saying is actually accurate from a factual standpoint.

Do not be just an employee but learn to have the mindset of both a shareholder and an employee. This doesn't mean you will never have challenges or be laid off, but having this mindset will allow you at least be able to see where your company is actually going and help you better position yourself to help your company reach its full potential. In some cases, that knowledge might make you decide to part ways when you realize the necessary changes are not being made to keep up with a changing world and business model.

25. Financial defense protects your wealth

Change is one of only two constants in life (the other is death). Today, we experience change more rapidly. In this fast-moving financial landscape, it can feel overwhelming at times. You think you have a good business one day, but tomorrow the business idea is obsolete. That's how quickly it can happen. Since the world is moving faster than ever and what you know today could be invalid possibly in the next hour, how can you financially plan for you and those you love?

Two words: financial defense. In sports, it's commonly known that defense is what wins championships. In this new digital world, you have to ask yourself, how good is your financial defense?

You can create a financial defensive wall by continuously investing in yourself. Don't focus on what might be the next big thing because nobody knows. Instead, stay focused on increasing your knowledge by investing in your education. Learn to be flexible and adaptive to embrace and see potential opportunities that change might bring you. Stay on top of technology to better understand it and see how it could help you in the future. In short, continue to invest in yourself.

Investing your time and money to improve your financial defense is important for your long-term financial future. In all sports, you have to be able to stop the other team as well. But maintaining and strengthening your defense doesn't mean you can't play offense. Since you've spent the time to build up your financial defense, you're more likely to give yourself the best opportunity to win, and sometimes all you have to do is ensure the opponent doesn't score more than you.

A good defensive mindset is focusing on your mortgage debt rather than buying the right home that is certain to appreciate overtime or is most desirable. Whether home prices go up or down will have less of an impact on you as your focus was more on mortgage debt, which means you not only bought a home that you likely love but one that gave you some financial protection.

Develop a mindset that financial defense is what will create and protect wealth. Invest strategically in your financial defense, and always ask yourself: How good is my financial defense?

Be unapologetic about betting on yourself even when there is 100% certainty of your failure. It is much better to live a life knowing your failures were a result of your unapologetic belief in yourself than to live a life without failures.

CHAPTER 24

YOU ARE THE KEY

When my family and I moved from Nigeria to Canada, we met a couple whom my family referred to as our adopted grandparents, Lorne and Vernetta. There's something remarkable about the ability of strangers to love each other as though they were blood family members. At the time, I played soccer, and I joined a local community team in our area. While I was good at soccer, soccer wasn't really a popular sport in Canada at the time, especially where we moved to due to the harsh winter months.

Our adopted grandparents were spiritual and religious individuals, with their faith playing a strong role in how they moved through life. They shared a deep love for each other as both had been through their own life challenges. Their spirit reminds me of my mother's spirit, and I think that's why both of them really connected with my mother. The three of them shared a similar spirit in how they carried themselves through life. Lorne and Vernetta would bring us gifts during the holiday season, and we would go to their house for holidays and casual dinners. One day, Lorne pull me outside for a pretty honest conversation about the reality of my parents' financial situation in Canada.

He essentially told me that in Canada, people don't appreciate soccer yet, but basketball was something people did appreciate. He said he believed I could make the switch and be good at basketball. He said if I was able to do that and if I worked hard at it, I could get a scholarship from a school to pay for my university studies.

Then he proceeded to tell me something that would motivate me for my entire basketball career. He told me the reality is that my parents are extremely hard workers but given the system they were trying to learn and where they are in their life stage, it would be difficult for them to get ahead or pay for my school. He said I'd have to work hard at basketball and school to ensure I would secure a scholarship to give myself a chance to attend post-secondary school.

That conversation has stayed with me throughout my entire life. See, most people are afraid to be honest (including me at times) with those we love and even more so with strangers. It's hard to tell the truth to someone you love or care about because it takes two people to create a truth. One has to be willing to speak the truth, and the other has to be willing to hear and accept the truth. Lorne told me something important and truthful about my situation and my family's financial challenges in Canada that changed my life for the better that day. I listened and accepted his truth.

But equally as important, Lorne didn't only tell me the truth, he backed up his truth through his actions. He told me he would send me to a basketball camp and pay the fees associated with it. As he promised, he signed me up for a local summer camp with a college near me. He did this for the first few years, and it was amazing. I sucked at basketball when I started. I couldn't do a simple layup or dribble, but I kept trying.

I kept practicing because I knew he wanted me to be successful and was putting his money—and more importantly, his time—where his belief and heart was. I also knew he was absolutely right about my parent's financial situation. My parents were not going to be in a position to pay for my university studies, and I had to go to university.

As I played basketball, I always remembered the conversation with Lorne. Every time I stepped into the gym, I thought about it. I knew basketball was my ticket to college. I had to work harder than anyone to ensure that. I had to show people I was better than they were, but not only that: I was prepared to work harder than they were.

Most of those whom I played against were kids whose parents just wanted to keep them busy and have them do something productive. Some parents hoped their kids might became a star, but for most parents, paying for college was not an impossible task. They could get loans or perhaps they had saved up enough for their kid's post-secondary studies.

At first, these kids were better than I was because they had more practice. But I would continue to practice. I had a local basketball court about a 20-minute walk from my house, and I would go there pretty much every weekend and anytime during the week I could. I would practice my dribbling on the sidewalk in front of our house. I would do my pushups before going to bed. When I got to high school, I would go to the gym before class started. I did all those things because basketball was my ticket to an education. I worked hard because I knew in order to ensure my parents' sacrifice in moving to Canada wasn't a waste, I had to go to university. I had to make something of myself to be able to help them.

When I played against other kids, I realized they didn't have the same motivation as I did. Mine was just to get to college and have basketball pay my schooling. This deep motivation meant most people I played against couldn't match my drive. Those who were better than I was at the time just couldn't match my hunger.

Eventually, I gained some success, and my skill and talent started to be noticed. As my success grew, so did the discouragement. I heard people make up all sorts of reasons as to why I wasn't better. It was discouraging at times as most of them thought I didn't hear their comments, but I did. I am an extremely competitive person, and I just used it all as fuel. I learned to just keep smiling and stay focused on my goal. That focus would eventually land me a scholarship to attend post-secondary school.

Why do I tell this story? I tell it because everything I have written in this book means absolutely nothing if you do not choose to act on the information. Lorne spoke an important truth to me and provided me the initial investment to ensure I could be successful. Everything I have written in this book is to try and tell you my truth about housing and finance, and more specifically about mortgages as I have come to understand the way they work.

Not only have I told you my truth, but I've also provided you with some initial investment ideas. Listening to Lorne's truth wasn't what ultimately lead to my success in getting a university scholarship, though. At the end of the day, it was my work ethic, determination, and an unapologetic bet and belief in myself. I learned early that if I bet on myself then regardless of the result, I can't really lose. The most powerful tool most of us have isn't what we own or our income stream but rather our mind.

It's the tool most people allow others to take away from them by placing limitation and fear in your mind. Lorne wanted me to realize that it wasn't the sport that was my most powerful asset, it was my mind. If I could open my mind to the possibility of making the change from one sport to another, then it didn't matter if I got the scholarship, only that I was willing to change. He knew I would realize it was really my mind that was the key to my future.

I cannot stress enough that the key to improving your situation is you. The difference between individuals who are successful and those who want to be successful is their mindset approach to life, and more importantly, the actions they take to make that a reality. Successful people match their intentions with their behaviors. They don't need to spend time talking about what they want to do as they are already doing it. They don't talk about the life they wish they could live because they are already taking actions to live that life or are living it.

Purchasing a home is one of the biggest debts you will take on. I've provided you some knowledge to better inform yourself, but what you decide to do with the information is up to you. Therefore, the question isn't whether you can be successful, but rather are you prepared to do the things required to be successful? This book isn't meant to be the solution for you. It's my belief that the best way to truly help another human being isn't to provide them with the solution but rather to encourage them to see they are the solution to improving their situation.

Any success you have will not be the result of this book as this book might only account for 1%, if even that. You are the other 99% that will create your own success. This book is my investment in you as I believe you are capable of creating the life you desire. Only you can determine your own worth. Therefore, bet on yourself with every single breath you take in this life.

I wish you only the best, and I know if you're willing to work hard, you have all the skills and knowledge to be successful.

You are the key and the solution to improving your situation.

THANK YOU

No one obtains success on their own. While it's tempting to believe who I am today is a result of just my hard work, the reality is I had a lot of help along the way. Sure, I had to work hard, but my success isn't entirely a result of my actions only. I've been blessed in my life journey beyond my understanding to deal with and meet people who for unknown reasons stepped forward to move me forward in my life. I have mentioned two of my foundational supporters—my wife and family.

Success requires much more than just the support of those who care for you, however. For one to reach success in any form, they need others—even strangers—who then become like family. Some who had been strangers drove me to my basketball games even when they had their own family to take care of. They offered me free haircuts every time I needed one. They funded my basketball fees to ensure I could compete at the highest level possible. They talked to other coaches to ensure I got as much exposure as possible in order to land my scholarship. Some even let me keep my basketball track outfit when I didn't pay for it. They spoke to teachers on my behalf when I was struggling academically. And some offered their home for me to sleep and food for me to eat when needed. These strangers, who for reasons unknown to me, stepped up when I needed it. I wouldn't be who I am today without people who stepped up to support me in my life's journey. I owe them so much.

And with that in mind, I want to take a moment to just say thank you for purchasing this book.

You've now become a supporter of mine and continue to prove my belief that no one is successful on their own without others willing to lend a hand. As such, I want to offer a small token of appreciation to the first 100 of you who purchase this book. As a result of reading the book and reading this section, I will be providing a free one-hour financial coaching session to you to show my appreciation.

The offer will be on a first-come, first-served basis. To sign up, please visit: www.wealthmarathon.com and click the book tab. On the bottom of the page, you will see a form for financial coaching book offer. I will accept requests until the 100 quota has been hit. From there, I will provide you more details. I highly recommend that you take the free time to discuss financial matters as it will give you the most value. I encourage you to come prepared to discuss financial items about which you need honest feedback or things that are preventing you from betting on yourself. The free session is about you and not me.

Once again, thank you, and I wish you and those you love all the best in your life journey. Keep pushing forward, and always remember you are the key to improving whatever situation you are going through.

All my best,

Brighton

www.ingramcontent.com/pod-product-compliance
Lightning Source LLC
Chambersburg PA
CBHW031848200326
41597CB00012B/316